M000290739

"Come follow me, Jesus said, and I will make you fishers of men."

–Matthew 4:19

The Boat and the Sea of Galilee

Lea Lofenfeld and Ramit Frenkel

AN ARCHAEOLOGICAL GLIMPSE INTO THE WORLD OF JESUS

THE BOAT AND THE SEA OF GALILEE

Lea Lofenfeld and Ramit Frenkel

Translated from the Hebrew by Ora Cummings

gefen

publishing house בית הוצאה לאור

JERUSALEM ◆ NEW YORK

Copyright © Gefen Publishing House
Jerusalem 2007/5767

All rights reserved. No part of this publication may be translated, reproduced, stored in a retrieval system
or transmitted, in any form or by any means, electronic, mechanical, photocopying, recording or otherwise,
without express written permission from the publishers.

Layout: Marzel A.S. — Jerusalem
Cover Design: S. Kim Glassman

ISBN: 978-965-229-402-9

Edition   1 3 5 7 9 8 6 4 2

First printing: December 2007

Gefen Publishing House Ltd.
6 Hatzvi St., Jerusalem 94386, Israel
972-2-538-0247
orders@gefenpublishing.com

Gefen Books
600 Broadway, Lynbrook, NY 11563, USA
1-516-593-1234
orders@gefenpublishing.com

www.israelbooks.com

Printed in Israel

Send for our free catalogue

Contents

Acknowledgments

To Moshe Lofenfeld, the love of my life, and my best friend, without whom this book would not have come to fruition.

— *Lea Lofenfeld*

To our beloved family: Alex Frenkel, who helped with generosity and knowledge; Einat and Doron, who are wonderful; and all the special grandchildren: Iddan, Ori, Omer, Gali and Tal.

— *Lea and Ramit*

We would like to thank the following people:

The brothers Moshe and Yuval Lufan, who discovered the boat and followed its restoration to the special museum.

Nitza Kaplan, director of the Bet Allon Museum in Kibbutz Ginosar, for all her help.

Tovia Kurtz for his golden hands.

Ora Cummings, our literary agent, who always showed us the right way.

Sarah Sirota, Tamar Moritz, Tamar and Danny Razoumov for being there for us.

Akiva Pressman (z"l), who always offered help before being asked.

Ilan Greenfield of Gefen Publishing House, who believed in this book from the first moment he read it, and Gefen staff Smadar, Eitan and Dorit.

Special thanks to Prof.. Kurt Raveh for his introduction and belief in the boat.

Introduction:
The Emotional Cargo of An Ancient Boat

There she lies now, bathing under the spotlights of her own museum, our Galilee boat, resurrected from and forming a direct link to biblical times. Every time I look at her, high up in the air on her stainless steel support in her carefully air-conditioned and moisturized environment, she kind of amazes me again and again and gives me a glowing feeling deep within my heart and soul, as if she is thanking me for having been there, for helping to rescue her from obscurity, after being hidden there in her wet, cold and dark muddy tomb for two thousand years.

We were the fortunate ones, the first to lay eyes on her and to touch this ancient fishing boat, the only one to survive since the times of Joshua of Nazareth, hidden for twenty centuries in the world's holiest lake on that same site where those biblical events actually occurred, from the source of Christianity.

Sitting on the jetty adjacent to the Ginosar museum, enjoying the silence and the pastoral view over the Sea of Galilee, the flickering of the sunlight on the rippling waters triggers the memory of those first moments of discovery.

I never will forget the excitement and the feeling of inner fulfillment when we discovered the first mortise and tenon joints, oil lamps and cooking pot, giving us the archaeological data to prove we had a major Roman period find. Eureka! Personally, on that moment of that rainy January morning in 1982, wet and cold and covered in mud, I could feel by gently touching it, the "life"

About the writer: Kurt Raveh, maritime archaeologist and museologist, was with Shelley Wachsmann co-director of the Galilee Boat Excavation, with Orna Cohen taking charge of the boat's preservation. He is currently a research fellow in the University of Haifa's Department of Humanities and co-director along with Yaacov Kahanov and Chris Brandon of the NAS (International Nautical Archaeology Society). His discoveries, life and works have been featured in National Geographic and Discovery Channel documentaries.

in this ancient wood. This lady-ship had a soul and we all realized that our lives would never be the same after that day's events.

Whether this boat was used by Jesus himself, we will never be able to prove or disprove; all we can say is that it is from that time, that place and that moment in history. As the only archaeological relic of its kind, this boat was an exceptional find. All I can truly say as one of the directing archaeologists of the project is that even with thirty years experience and countless major discoveries and excavations of ancient shipwrecks under my belt — Napoleon's lost cannon, tells, tombs and treasure enough to make Hollywood's Indiana Jones jealous — this was undoubtedly the most extraordinary find of my career and I dare say of the twentieth century.

The excitement around the project was immediate: the boat was already famous the world over while still being excavated and discovered. Never have I been on an excavation which was already a crowded tourist site, with hot dog stands and ice cream vendors.

Having to be protected by police and army guards, with every move recorded by dozens of international TV crews, was a novel experience for me, but the benefit was that this was probably one of the best recorded excavations ever. How can I possibly explain where all the equipment, help and volunteers came from, the people feeding us, the site crowded with advice and help

from foreign ambassadors, military and clergy, kibbutzniks and local farmers and fishermen, each contributing in his or her own way.

Afterwards we lectured the world over about this amazing boat, meeting famous diplomats and world leaders. Of all of these encounters I especially treasure the moment when the two main heroes of this saga, the Jewish fisherman kibbutz brothers Moshele and Yuval Lufan, who discovered the boat, accompanied me to the first official visit of a Pope to the Holy Land ever, in the magic year of 2000 CE, and to the ceremony on the nearby Mount of Beatitudes.

How can I ever explain how we managed to overcome every major problem of digging out an ancient waterlogged boat 212 meters below the level of the Mediterranean Sea on the bottom of the world's deepest sweet-water lake? How can one understand the confluence of miracles that had to come together for this boat to emerge whole from the sea, beginning with the water level that allowed us to execute a dry land excavation?

How did we manage to keep this waterlogged boat from falling apart while it was hardly holding up its own weight? How on earth did we resurrect this boat in one piece out of her muddy tomb and make it float again over the lake's waters after two thousand years?

How did we again and again come up with creative and immediate solutions, such as using on-site cactus needles when we needed something "nature friendly" to stick the tags on the wooden planks and frames, or Moshele's invention of using fish to fight the worms and parasites that threatened certain destruction of the boat while in the sweet-water holding tank?

In short, how was this unprepared, underfunded and under-equipped rescue excavation project completed in a record eleven days, when the salvage of another ancient wreck of about the same size in the Mediterranean Sea was a five-year event?

And finally how, after ten years of being "cooked" in sixty tons of preservation fluid, did the boat emerge again out of the murky deeps still in one piece, crowning the efforts of our preservations hero, Orna?

All I can say today is that it was due to the total dedication of the salvation crew and a little help from our friends; for the rest we just proved that miracles still do happen here, as they did back then.

I came to Israel for three weeks, and I've stayed for more than thirty years. With Shelley Wachsmann I created a base of operations in an old glass factory, and together we've discovered dozens of other wreck sites in the Mediterranean Sea, mainly at the ancient site of Dor, near Caesarea. Recently we discovered here an underwater site dating to the times of the kings, David and Solomon. And who knows what else awaits us. But one thing we know for sure: nothing will top this "Jesus Boat" adventure, ever!

For us personally, no fortunes were made out of this world famous discovery, but it certainly enriched and forever changed the lives of all of us, the "band of boat-brothers." Because this ancient boat carried no treasure but a special spiritual, sentimental and above all, emotional cargo. And with it the message of brotherhood and peace, AMAZING GRACE,

AMEN.

— Kurt Raveh
Christmas 2007

Come follow me, Jesus said, and I will make you fishers of men.

— Matthew 4:19

Jesus Christ: The medeity and humanity, the junction of heaven and earth.

— Anonymous

Part One

The Boat

Prologue: Key to the Gate of Dreams

Sometimes, at night, Moshe and Yuval grasped at dreams, touched ancient treasures and collected gold coins.

Sometimes, at night, Moshe and Yuval saw fearless knights driving away cruel, mercenary robbers.

Almost from the moment they first opened their eyes to the world, Moshe and Yuval knew for certain that one day they would find a treasure. Perhaps it would be a tightly bound leather bundle full of gold coins, or some ancient treasure dropped from the deck of a ship by a frightened sailor, or an ancient gold goblet, last seen in Leonardo De Vinci's painting of the Last Supper, thought to have disappeared forever.

And here, one day in late December 1985, the two brothers, Moshe and Yuval Lufan, from Kibbutz Ginosar on the coast of the Kinneret (the Hebrew name for the Sea of Galilee), took a walk to the ancient port of Magdala, to swim in the "bitter" waters that flowed from Magdala into the big inland lake. On their last dive, Moshe's hand suddenly touched something hard. He touched it, deep in the water, feeling the outline of the object that had aroused his curiosity. Night had already fallen over the coast and Moshe sensed that the object he had found was covered by a very thick layer of silt and mud. He grabbed hold of Yuval and the two hurried back to the kibbutz. At the gate, they met Claire, the archaeologist, and handed over their find to be evaluated.

Early the following morning, as they took their places in the communal kibbutz dining room, Claire materialized and wordlessly held a closed fist out toward them, on a level with their eyes. She opened her fist and…Moshe and Yuval were almost blinded. On the archaeologist's open palm lay an exquisite key, sending out glorious sparks of light. It might have been seen as just a key, or perhaps a golden goblet, or a knight, flanked on either side by angels; on the other hand, it might even have been an early omen that this was the key to the gates of their dreams.

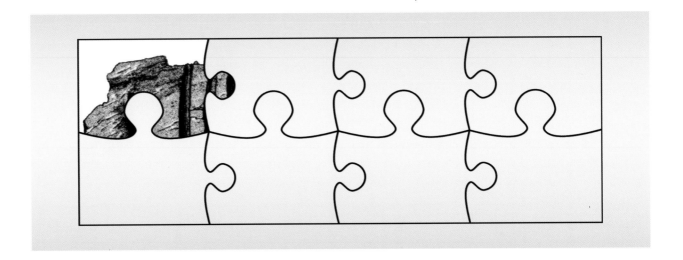

Chapter One

The Poor Widow's Mites

One dark and dingy night, a week before the beginning of the excavation, in late January 1986, a military truck was making its way along the coast of the Sea of Galilee, very close to the water's edge. None of the passengers on board had the slightest inkling of the fact that a number of sweet-water springs were bubbling away very near the surface of the water. Suddenly, some unseen hand seemed to have forced its way up out of the wet ground and grabbed the military truck, which sunk down into the darkness to a depth of almost one meter. The soldiers who jumped down to rescue the truck only succeeded in making it sink even deeper.

The truck grunted and groaned and seemed almost to choke to death, as if it were some helpless, heavy-bodied animal begging to be rescued from the swamp. The truck driver, on whose conscience lay the entire weight of his truck, walked around and around the sinking vehicle, trying to figure out any possible way to save it. As a last resort, he grabbed a wireless receiver, called base and asked for assistance. The backup truck arrived quite quickly and the noise it made woke Moshe, who alerted Yuval, and the two peeped out from behind their closed curtains. After no more than a few minutes even the rescued truck joined the happy cheers.

The following day, even before the first rays of light, Yuval and Moshe set out to examine the spot at which the army truck had been stuck in Kinneret mud. And, indeed, their hopes were not dashed. The truck's spinning wheels and the stamping of the soldiers' boots in the soft earth had brought to the surface a number of small coins. Yuval was the first of the two to bend down and when he straightened up and opened his hand a coin was cradled in it. When he wiped away the sand and mud that was stuck to the coin the two were thrilled by what they saw. One side of the

The poor widow's mites

coin was engraved with an eight-pointed star, a faded Greek letter between each point. Moshe's breath caught, and Yuval screeched like a chick taking to the air for the first time.

Moshe, who must have been the first to retrieve his faculties, flipped over the coin and there on its other side was an engraving of a ship's anchor, surrounded by barely discernible Greek letters. As if gripped by fever, they dropped to the ground, digging, turning over clumps of earth, quickly at first, then slowly, more cautiously, and suddenly they were both screeching and pulling out more and more coins and, in their excitement, dripping with sweat and whispering over the metal discs, they were disappointed only that the person who

had struck them had not managed to make them more perfectly round.

Finally the two brothers, whose entire world was more sea than land, stood up, holding the coins, looking as if bewitched at the anchor engraved on one side. The sight had simply stepped out of their dreams. As usual they ran straight to Claire, who would identify and describe and send the treasure to the Department of Antiquities (since 1990 known as the Israel Antiquities Authority) in Jerusalem. And Claire, the archaeologist who had immigrated from England and settled in Kibbutz Ginosar, where she accompanied and educated the children in how to deal with archaeological finds, scrutinized the coins and scrutinized the brothers and sensed the excitement flowing from the coins to the brothers and from the brothers back to her.

She told them that these coins were minted in the days of King Alexander Jannaeus (103–76 BCE) and that they were known as "poor widow's mites." And she went on to tell them that these coins are mentioned in the New Testament, in the story of the widow's offering. They set out in search of the story in the scriptures, and this is what they found:

> He sat down opposite the treasury, and watched the crowd putting money into the treasury. Many rich people put in large sums. A poor widow came and put in two small copper coins, which are worth a penny. Then he called his disciples and said to them, "Truly, I tell you, this poor widow has put in more than all those who are contributing to the treasury. For all of them have contributed out of their abundance; but she out of her poverty has put in every-thing she had, all she had to live on."
>
> *(Mark 12:41–44)*

It was engraved onto the tablets of their hearts in letters of fire, and they actually experienced the sense of righteousness that accompanies real giving, the kind that comes from within.

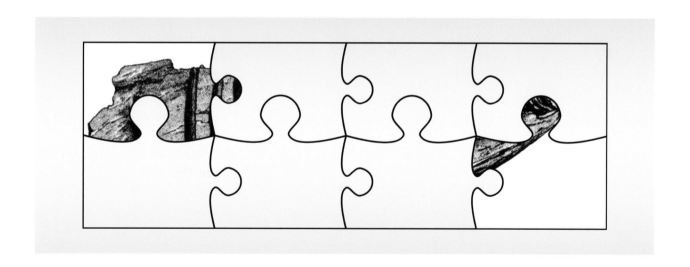

First-century CE mosaic found near Migdal

THE BOAT AND THE SEA OF GALILEE

The Boat

One week after finding the poor widow's mites, Yuval and Moshe, the two brothers who always follow their hearts, returned to the same spot where they had found the coins, and some inner urge drove them to bend down and start digging and delving. And then…then came the discovery, the realization of a dream, a dream they had been dreaming all their lives…

The years 1983, 1984 and 1985 were drought years; there was no rainfall and the sun gulped up large drafts from the Sea of Galilee.

The Sea of Galilee is the main source of water in the Land of Israel and the entire population of the country kept a fearful eye on the water level as it escaped inward from its shoreline and shrank away.

During that time, the two brothers, Moshe and Yuval Lufan, were concerned, just like everyone else in the country, but they were also discomfited by a strange happiness dancing about deep in their hearts. They hid their happiness, confused and ashamed that the dropping water line represented for everyone else a pressing fear while their own hearts were filled with joy. But they were unable to overcome this joy. They both knew that as the Kinneret shrank, new shores and new depths would be revealed, which for thousands of years had been covered with water. Here, now, they would be able to excavate those shores and maybe even expose such treasures as no man's eye had gazed upon in thousands of years.

Now Moshe and Yuval walked, bent over, along the shore, breathing heavily, burrowing with trembling fingers at every indent in the sand and hoping. They made their way to the coast, whose escaping waters had revealed a new shoreline. They sensed every tiny stone, trying with a light touch to detect what kind of object they had touched. Suddenly a sharp cry cut through the silence and was replaced, once again, by silence. Yuval looked at his brother, his face awash with sweat, his eyes shining with a thousand stars. His hands were deep in the damp sand, his mouth unable to utter a word. Very slowly, he removed his hands from the sand and opened them; Yuval's eyes opened wide at the sight of the ancient sand-covered coins.

Not a word was said. The two exchanged glances. Yuval bit his lips, as a light wind blew in from the sea and dried the streams of sweat on their faces. They bent down, continuing to dig carefully, moving slowly along the beach, careful not to miss so much as a single millimeter. And Yuval's finger encountered something small, hard and…sharp. Carefully, Yuval removed his hand and cleaned away the silt that had stuck to the object and the two whispered voicelessly to each other what only the Sea of Galilee could hear: "an ancient nail!"

And now they were both digging gingerly, but the ancient nail had fired their imaginations and they dug, making a deeper dent in the sand, and suddenly Yuval's finger was pricked again and another ancient nail peeped up at him. The two looked at each other and, with the excitement that was burning within them all the time, they dug inch by inch and here, in front of their astounded

eyes, from beneath a layer of silt there emerged the blurred outline of a strake, a single breadth of a boat's planking from stem to stern.

And they wanted to shout at the tops of their voices, to jump high in the air, to touch the skies, but all they were able to do was to breathe again, to bite their lips and, once more, they were bending over and continuing to clean away the mud, to remove it carefully, to scratch it away, very, very slowly. They barely dared to touch, using only their fingertips, and the edge of another ancient plank, a wooden strake, was revealed…

The two brothers hugged each other, only their lips moving. No sound came out as they mouthed, "…ancient…"

They looked at each other in disbelief, their faces streaked with mud, but quickly composed themselves and covered the spot where the upper line of the strake had revealed itself, blurring any signs of a dig, covering over the indents, raking over with their fingers any sign that might give away their find. Then they ran off to their father.

As soon as they came to their father and he looked into their eyes, he understood everything.

They linked arms, all three of them, and returned to the dig. They looked in all directions before exposing the strake again. And their father stood, silently watching, saying nothing, carefully looking all around. Seeing no one, he relaxed and knelt down, touching with utmost caution; not

An ancient boat discovered in the Sea of Galilee

saying a word, he rose, moved to the other side and knelt down again. He carefully exposed some more of the upper strake, but continued to say nothing. Moshe and Yuval, who were holding their breath without even realizing it throughout their father's examination, suddenly began breathing once again as their father Yanky broke his long silence.

"Let's expose a tiny little bit more, but it seems to me that this wooden plank has been sunk for so many years in such deep water that the mud and silt that have adhered to it have become a part of it. And if you look really closely, only at the upper strake that is exposed, you'll agree with me that it really does look like something that belongs to a fishing boat. And we haven't heard of any such boat sinking recently, which reinforces the assumption that this plank is a part of the wooden structure of an ancient boat." And now these words that had been following the two brothers all the days and nights of their lives had been spoken, and they knew that their father could not be mistaken, for he is the sort who speaks only when absolutely certain of what he is saying.

And the skies went dizzy above them and it even seemed to them that the earth was spinning beneath their feet, and Yuval's head started to spin also, and he would have fallen had his little brother Moshe not managed to grab him and steady him on his feet.

Their excitement grew, communicated only in barely audible whispers; everything remained top secret, passed on only by word of mouth and in the most clandestine manner. A foreign marine archaeologist was brought in and he examined the find and said nothing. When he opened his mouth to speak, a kind of coldness emanated from between his teeth and dropped the two brothers' hearts into the abyss, or even lower. But the truth was that neither of them believed a word of what he had to say.

"This," he said, "is an almost brand new boat, a couple of hundred years old, at the most…"

And every word, as it fell on their ears, weighed at least a ton and rolled on down into the Sea of Galilee.

For two whole weeks the two brothers wandered around their kibbutz, their heads bowed to the ground. They saw no one, neither friends nor relatives. And then, when the two weeks were up, one early evening, without even discussing it between them, without planning or arranging to meet, a new spirit visited them and their feet led them to the front door of Nitza's home (Nitza Kaplan, the manager of the Yigal Allon Center). No one inside heard the two knocking on the door and Moshe opened it carefully. The two fell upon all the commotion of a family evening meal. There they all were sitting around a large table, eating and drinking, totally oblivious of Moshe and Yuval standing in the doorway. The brothers were embarrassed and thought, "Are we invisible?"

And then it was Moshe, the more bashful of the two, who suddenly found himself gently tapping Nitza's shoulder and, incredibly, leading her just a little bit firmly into the other room. And Moshe did not stop talking with Nitza, who, from the very beginning, was gesticulating, waving her hands excitedly in the air: "No," she said and "no" again, and her whole being was saying "no!" But Moshe kept talking until she raised one of her hands and Yuval and Moshe heard her whispering a name: "Mendel Nun."

It was the same Mendel Nun of Kibbutz En Gev who, many years before when their father, Yanky, had just arrived on the shores of the Kinneret, made a point of meeting him, and the two spent many a day fishing in the big lake. Mendel was enchanted by the lake and went on to learn everything there is to know about marine archaeology at the university, where he got lost among the books. But every time anyone called to ask for his help, Mendel would emerge from between the tomes and make his way back to the Kinneret. And Mendel, on the phone, could sense Nitza's excitement before the brothers had had a chance to add so much as a word to her story, and he immediately appeared.

They waited for him at their father's home,

and the level of excitement rose and put an end to any conversation. Together, they set out to the site, in near silence. Carefully, in a way that was almost sacred, they began digging, and the strake revealed itself once again. Mendel remained seated, his hands clearing away the sand, almost stroking the old plank, and he was still silent, his eyes downcast a little longer, digging deeper to expose more. And then, in spite of the storm within him he managed to say: "Friends, this is an ancient boat! We must call in the Department of Antiquities."

And for the first time in his life, Moshe understood the full meaning of the words "spiritual uplift."

Moshe and Yuval made their way back over the kibbutz pathways, their feet stepping on the ground, but their spirits floating somewhere up there above their heads.

Yuval and his oldest brother Benny often go dancing in the large dining rooms of the neighboring kibbutzim, and this is exactly what they did that same evening. The hall was filled to overflowing with dancing couples. Yuval, who was dressed all in white, danced alone, his spirit floating over everyone else. The following morning, when Benny saw him, he laughed: "Yuval, it's just as well that the kibbutz dining room has a roof. Otherwise, who's to tell where you would have floated off to?"

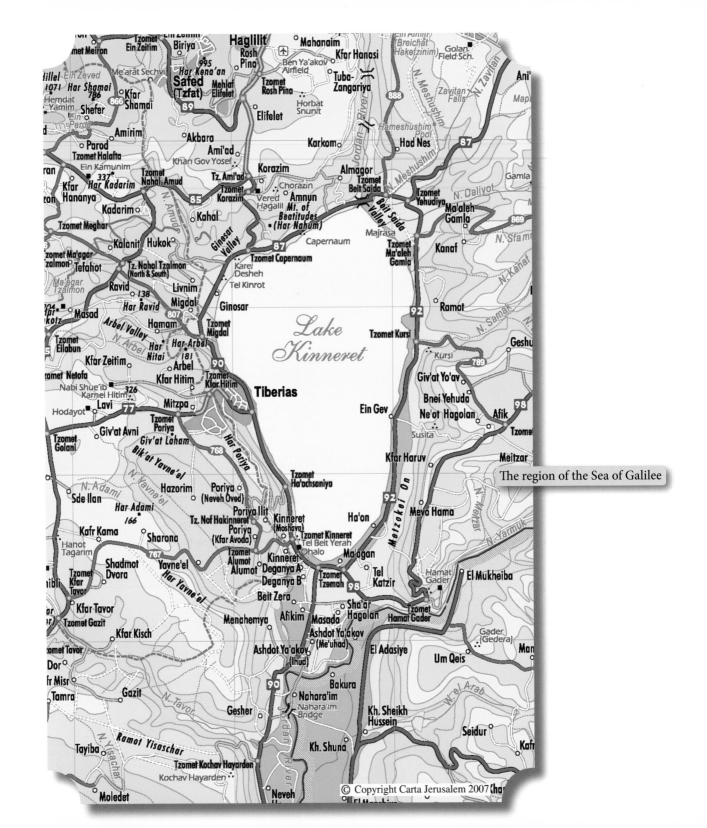

The region of the Sea of Galilee

© Copyright Carta Jerusalem 2007

A Double Rainbow in the Sky

The spiritual uplift and determination that had infused Yuval and Moshe must have attached themselves to the message they sent to the Department of Antiquities and the museums. Professor Shelley Wachsmann and Dr. Kurt Raveh arrived at the Lufan household on the wings of this excitement. They turned up in a jeep laden down with state-of-the-art deep sea diving equipment, the last word in wet suits and oxygen tanks, medical equipment and the latest photographic equipment for regular and underwater photography. Shelley Wachsmann and Kurt Raveh emerged from the jeep, charged and full of energy.

"Where exactly do we have to dive in order to locate the boat?" they asked. When Yuval explained that the Kinneret occasionally moves away from its shores and the boat was actually on dry land, they opened their mouths so wide that they almost forgot to close them.

Four people made their way full of excitement toward the treasure. On their way, the two marine archaeologists, Shelley and Kurt, explained that if it transpired that the ship's planks were connected to each other by a joining system known as mortise and tenon construction, then this would indicate that it was most certainly an ancient boat. Beginning with the second century BCE and until the first centuries CE, this was the method used by boat-wrights in this part of the Mediterranean Sea for joining planks to each other.

The two brothers thought, "mortise and tenon," and tried to turn the strange words into a joke, in an attempt to release some of the tension within them, but then they realized that it is quite hard to joke with excited archaeologists whose internal compass needles are trembling with anticipation because of a magnetic field from another dream.

The four arrived at the site of the boat, which

of course was known only to the two brothers, and the digging began once again. Again, the upper strake was revealed. Shelley and Kurt bent down and began smoothing away the sand, inch by inch, going a little deeper, carefully, to reveal the other plank and examine the joint, touching them, looking at each other and suddenly the two grown men, sane and sober, were up on their feet, linking arms, raising their legs up in the air, dancing to some inner rhythm, their lips moving in a silent whisper.

The two brothers were watching them, understanding what was happening here, the meaning of the strangled, intoxicating little dance, but wanting to hear the secret coded words, and the two brothers tried to grab the hems of the dancers' clothes, to halt the dance for a moment, and they begged, "Tell us, tell us!" And the two distinguished dancers heard nothing and were oblivious to everything that was happening around them, but continued whispering and dancing and suddenly the two archaeologists opened their arms and all four men danced together. By now, the two brothers were able to hear the secret code and together the four danced and whispered: "Mortise and tenon…mortise and tenon…mortise and tenon…"

And the taut skies above them, which for three years had held back the rains, opened up all seven gates to heaven and giant drops of water began to fall, drumming down, increasing in volume and growing in strength. That same rain that everyone had been praying for for three years, and here it came, all at once.

They were sure that they were back in the days of Noah's flood. But although the skies had dropped on them and water was streaming from their shirts and into their shoes and even out of their ears, they stood there joyful and wet in the huge puddle. All of a sudden, as quickly as it had started, the deluge stopped and only the streams of water still flowing down their faces and into their clothes and shoes bore witness to the heavy downfall just half a minute before.

Still reeling from the storm and the silence that followed it, they raised their eyes to the sky and, from behind the clouds, a pale yellow sun peeked down at them, it too a little shaken by the storm, the likes of which it had not seen for quite some time. And then from one edge of the skies across to their very end, the sun drew a magnificent double rainbow, brilliant in color, signaling that this was the very boat that the two Lufan brothers had been chosen to find and reveal and preserve and to show to the entire world.

All four stood in the middle of the silence that had fallen upon the world after the great storm and held their breath, and the entire universe held its breath with them. The wind did not blow, no waves broke on the sea and no bird made a sound in one of those rare moments in which you can almost hear the silence. They gazed up at the double rainbow which had in an instant colored their sky with so great and powerful a promise.

The four were gripped by a great emotion and without feeling it, they moved closer to each other, looking at each other, for a moment grasping each other, and from out of that same excitement that they all shared, they raised their arms to the skies and Moshe and Yuval whispered to the waves of the Sea of Galilee:

We pledge
Against the sea and the skies
To protect, to preserve and to treasure
This ancient boat.
And to reveal it, intact,
So it can be seen by
Everyone who lives on this earth!

And each of the four held his tongue and no one knows how it became known and how it happened, since in fact, not one of the four so much as whispered a hint, not a word, not even a syllable, not a letter — nothing was said. But rumors have a habit of spreading on their own. And this rumor, too, began to roll, first as a closely kept secret, from one mouth to another ear, but gradually it grew in intensity, grew strong and rolled and spread and then it lost all connection to the truth and to reality and people who were close to the two brothers and people

The promise of the double rainbow

who were complete strangers began phoning them from the furthest reaches of the country to ask if it was true that they had unearthed an ancient pirate ship, with a tall ceramic jug hidden deep in its belly, full almost to the rim with gold coins.

And in the wake of the rumors and the stories, people started turning up from all over the place — people whose childhoods had been colored by stories of daredevil pirates, robbers of the high seas. They started stealing in on foot, or in cars, carrying rakes and shovels and forks and the more audacious among them even arrived on tractors and Moshe and Yuval found themselves facing the crowd and swearing by everything that is dear to them that they had found no gold coins, neither belonging to robbers of the high sea, nor to Turks. But inside, deep down inside, the worries and fears grew stronger.

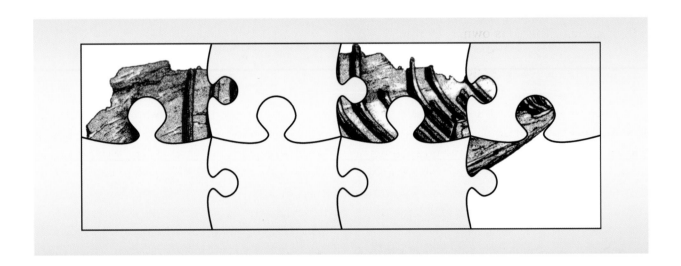

Chapter Four

The Migdalites

Near Kibbutz Ginosar, there remain the ruins of the ancient town of Magdala (called "Tarichaeae" in Greek). Of the old settlement only a very few ruins remain but the name survived until 1948, in the Arab village of Majdal, and until today in the nearby Jewish settlement, Migdal. An archaeological dig on the site of ancient Migdal revealed the remains of ancient buildings. The site of ancient Migdal is owned by the Church of the Franciscans, and two Franciscan monks excavated this site between 1971 and 1977. Today the site is closed and fenced in.

In the Franciscan dig, the remains of a Byzantine monastery were found, with rooms that had mosaic floors in patterns that include geometric symbols and crucifixes. A water reservoir was revealed to the west of the monastery. Through the ancient town a spring flows, alongside which a six-meter-high (19.7 ft.) square tower (a *migdal* in Hebrew) stands to this day. Scientists have

dated the town to the late Roman period. Two streets were unearthed next to the tower, one going north-south and the other in an east-west direction. One of the streets is paved with tiles in basalt and was dated to the Roman period. A six-meter-wide Roman road, unusually wide for the time period, was also discovered. To the east of the road, the archaeologists discovered the remains of three houses, one of them an elegant residential building, with an atrium and a central pool.

Another building complex was revealed, consisting of twenty-four rooms (see sketch of site E), pipes and two pools. To the south, a nine-hundred-square-meter town center was exposed; this was almost square and covered with perfectly chiseled sheets of basalt, surrounded by a lobby that measures 30.3×31.2 meters (99.4×102.4 ft), also tiled with chiseled basalt, not all of which has been preserved. Among the buildings' foun-

dations, the diggers found coins that had been minted between the period of the first century BCE and the first century CE. North of the spring-house, the diggers found a mosaic floor from the first century CE; at its center, there is an image of a wooden boat.

The ancient boat depicted in the mosaic is one of the only available realistic replicas of a Sea of Galilee fishing boat, and the mosaic was constructed at around the same time that the boat found by the Lufan brothers actually sailed on the Sea of Galilee.

The people of Magdala were well known for their courage and steadfastness. Josephus Flavius

Excavation on the Sea of Galilee — the first day

in the archaeological excavations in Magdala awakened in them the sense that this boat might belong to them.

When this rumor reached the ears of Moshe and Yuval, they already knew which way the wind was blowing in Migdal. Moshe quickly went to check that the site of the boat was well and truly described their love of liberty; they were the first to take a stand against the mighty Roman Empire.

When rumors reached the modern-day Migdalites that an ancient boat had been found in the Kinneret, their imagination was inflamed and, together with it, the legend was reawakened of a Turkish boat bearing a cargo of money to pay the salaries of the Turkish armies that were stationed in the Holy Land (which, until the second decade of the twentieth century, had been a part of the Turkish Ottoman Empire). According to the legend, the Turkish ship had sunk into the depths of the Sea of Galilee. The Migdalites immediately donned a new enthusiasm — maybe the mosaic of the ancient boat that was unearthed covered, but still, a sense of unease gnawed at him from inside. Fearing the "creative" ideas of the Migdalites, he ran off to the kibbutz cow sheds and appropriated a tractor, attaching a huge rake to it to cover up all signs of the site. Then he made his way to another spot, as far as possible from the site of the boat, and drew out an outline of an ancient boat, in order to mislead all those who were on the lookout for "their" boat. He then returned to the boat site and sprinkled more sand all around; then he went back to his kibbutz room and tried to sleep.

But his sleep was fitful and even before dawn, he got up and was horrified to see the Migdalites with two tractors and a dumper, surrounded by a solid human chain of Migdalites, each holding the hand of the person next to him, threatening any stranger who dared to approach them. When Moshe and Yuval's friend Dr. Claire Epstein, one of the senior archaeologists, went up to the Migdalite diggers, she returned pale and shaken. For the first time in her life, a rifle had been pointed at her in the course of an archaeological dig, with a finger on the trigger.

She was totally unused to such behavior among archaeologists. And now, Someone way above all the rest felt the fear and anxiety of the two brothers and saw the chain of Migdalites surrounding the spot and began immediately to collect some big black clouds at the edges of the skies, and Moshe and Yuval were terrified that the rains would harm the ancient boat.

The skies grew darker and more menacing and Moshe and Yuval felt helpless and frightened and hurriedly telephoned the Sea of Galilee Administration and asked, almost in a whisper, "Is it possible, perhaps, for the sake of preserving the boat intact, to open the dam at the River Jordan entrance to the Sea of Galilee, in order for the water level of the sea…to drop…" And on the other end of the telephone line, there was total silence.

In the offices of the Sea of Galilee Administration, they were absolutely certain that something had gone wrong in Moshe Lufan's thinking processes. Everyone knew that the water level of the Sea of Galilee had dropped perilously low, and everyone knows that the water level of the Sea of Galilee and the level of the nation's frame of mind are inextricably entwined. Who would dare ask to lower the water level of the Sea of Galilee?

But in the Holy Land, as in many other good places all over the world, we know that anything is possible if you have the right connections.

Even as the telephone in the Sea of Galilee Administration office was receiving two additional, extremely tense voices — those of Professor Shelley Wachsmann and Dr. Kurt Raveh — begging, literally begging, the director to do the impossible, there came the sound of engines and of heavy equipment. And Avi Eitan, who was then director of the Department of Antiquities, arrived and declared that the excavation site of the ancient boat was closed to everyone not involved in the dig. The police were called, as were the border police. And the Migdalites stood there watching in disbelief.

In the skies, dark, menacing clouds continued to accumulate over the Sea of Galilee. Heavy equipment vehicles arrived at the site, together with a delegation of "good souls." True, they still hadn't recovered from the request to open the dam, but with a speed that was unprecedented in this country, they managed to construct a strong, tall and stable dyke around the excavation site, and the *Sharqiya*, that strong, powerful wind which was already mustering its strength and making its way toward them, was apparently confused by the dyke and simply stopped in its tracks and dropped into the water near the excavation. Moshe and Yuval and all the others began the job of exposing the ancient boat.

The Migdalites, who were good at working a fiddle, realized that the boat in question was not the ship of gold left behind by the Turks, and wasted no time setting up a new source of income for them selves. They blocked off all the roads leading to the archaeological site and set up their own tollbooths, where they sold tickets that allowed entrance to these very same roads. And people flowed in from far and wide and when they became hungry and thirsty, they bought sandwiches and bottles of soft drinks at the mobile kiosks set up by the enterprising Migdalites.

But if you visit Midgal and ask anyone there if this is true, every Migdalite will roll his eyes to the sky and say: "What, me? I wasn't even there! Maybe, just maybe, my next-door neighbor was, though."

The two Lufan brothers, Moshe and Yuval, who discovered the ancient boat

Orna Cohen, conservationist

The Digging Begins

The initial examination was conducted by Professor Shelley Wachsmann and Dr. Kurt Raveh, after which the Department of Antiquities were convinced that the boat was indeed ancient, and swiftly organized themselves for the excavation. Wachsmann and Raveh stayed on site, where they were soon joined by Orna Cohen the conservationist, whose story is a wonder in itself.

In the Holy Land, there had never been any professional conservationists who specialized in conserving ancient boats. Yet suddenly and for no apparent reason, a year before the Kinneret boat appeared on the scene, the Department of Antiquities had welcomed home a charming young conservationist, Orna Cohen. Two years prior to the discovery of the Galilee boat, Orna Cohen had been led by some mysterious force to reach what appeared to be a strange decision — that it might be a good idea to enroll in the University of London in order to study the conservation of

boats. It would be even more worthwhile, she thought, to specialize in boat conservation in the laboratories of the British Museum.

With the instantly assembled team complete, the excavation began! That very night, Kibbutz Ginosar members and their friends started appearing from all directions. One came carrying an electricity generator; another arrived with several oil lamps; from the kibbutz kitchens, thermos flasks full of hot coffee materialized at the site, followed closely by women (still covered with flour) bearing trays of fragrant, freshly baked cakes and cookies. The kibbutz secretary appeared that same night, carrying a list of volunteers, all asking to be allowed to join the excavation at all hours and for any job, however menial. This infectious, never-ending volunteer spirit, which emanated from the heart, is but one of a long series of miracles that made possible the excavation and conservation of the boat.

In order to protect the boat, the mud was removed by hand

It is a well-known fact that materials such as metal that are subject to powerful movement — like the wings of an airplane, for instance — suffer from fatigue. Yes, materials can suffer fatigue, but the people of Kibbutz Ginosar, who were subject to a powerful emotional upheaval, felt no fatigue and were willing to volunteer for the excavation-revelation at all times of the day or night.

Moshe and Yuval, who all their lives had been drawn as if by magic to dig deep down into the earth's surface in order to connect with the past, had accumulated much knowledge regarding the excavation of a wooden boat, without understanding where from.

The fact is that no group of divers anywhere in the world had ever discovered a wooden boat that had been buried deep in sweet water for two thousand years. No archaeologists or divers possessed the kind of experience that could be of use in this case, but in the land of wonders and miracles, Moshe and Yuval had only to think and a huge light filled their heads, their sight became suddenly clear and they immediately understood the danger that might put the boat in jeopardy and what they had to do to expose it to the light of day without harming it; they knew how to preserve this unique boat to make it available to generations to come. It is amazing how many real hazards that could have seriously harmed the boat were avoided because of the "fish heads" that had grown on the shoulders of each of the brothers.

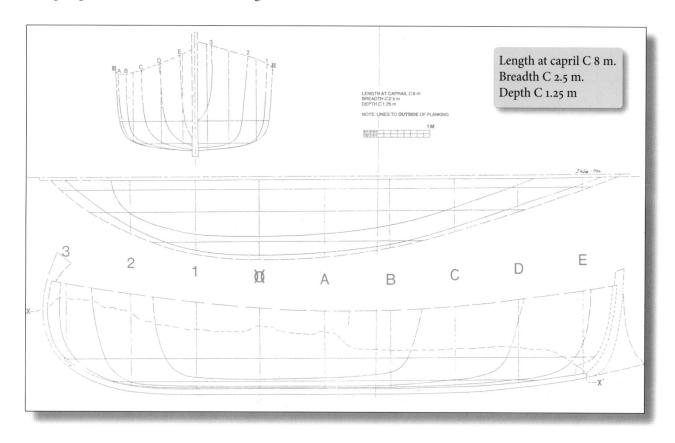

Length at capril C 8 m.
Breadth C 2.5 m.
Depth C 1.25 m

LENGTH AT CAPRAIL C 8 m
BREADTH C 2.5 m
DEPTH C 1.25 m

NOTE: LINES TO OUTSIDE OF PLANKING

1M

The excavation took place over days and nights and the volunteering spirit prevailed. Sometimes it was so great that the diggers actually felt as if they had lost their breath. They worked on the treasure, only their fingertips touching the wooden boards, carefully, lightly, barely touching, barely wiping away sand between thumb and forefinger, the wind blowing in lovingly, out of a sense of sanctity.

"Already, by the second night," Yuval said later, "the diggers were joined by Yochai, a childhood friend of Moshe's, who was also a fisherman and the son of a fisherman. I looked at him and noticed that Yochai was actually trembling when his hands touched the wooden plank. Yochai turned his gaze at me and breathed with difficulty. He told me that the moment he had touched the wood, he experienced a kind of slightly hallucinatory feeling, as if a stranger's fingers were returning his touch. Yochai actually felt the fingers of the carpenter who had built the boat. He was shocked for a moment, but soon pulled himself together and knew that even if the excavation was hard work, we'd succeed in getting it out intact."

Moshe and Yuval looked at each other when Yochai said this, smiling to each other and thinking: try telling a childhood friend that this is something they had known all along.

In the powerful sea of emotions and excite-ment, a great number of things happened at the very start of the excavation.

About half an hour after the dig began, when the uppermost strake was already

The fisherman's lamp found inside the boat and the ceramic pot found outside the boat near the prow

completely exposed, Moshe looked at it and could actually imagine how the entire boat would look. He stood up and began to stride along the length of the exposed strake, measuring its length with his steps and calculating, trying to estimate the approximate length of the boat.

According to his calculations, the boat was about eight meters in length. And then, according to the angle of the inward facing bow, Moshe tried to calculate the boat's width and he worked out that it would be about two and a quarter meters. Once the excavation was over, it became clear how accurate Moshe's calculations had been: it was

8.20 meters long and 2.3 meters wide (26.9×7.5 ft.). He had managed to work all this out when only the boat's uppermost strake was visible.

When the boat's uppermost strake was completely exposed, Moshe stood up once again and walked along to the other end and then he "stepped out" of the boat, and began digging in the sand outside the boat, very close to the area in which the boat's prow lay. Bent over, Moshe's hands slipped into the sand, digging carefully, until, suddenly, he stopped, his body turned to stone. Yuval, who was still digging inside the body of the boat, stopped, hopped "out" and ran to his brother. Carefully he helped Moshe clear the sand away and together they pulled out an ancient ceramic cooking pot.

The brothers were familiar with this kind of cooking utensil from previous excavations in which they had taken part, and they knew that such pots were used between the first century BCE and the first century CE. But they knew, nonetheless, that the ceramic pot could not be used in dating the period in which the boat had been built. Indeed, the ceramic pot had been found in the vicinity of the boat, but outside it, and it could well be that it was only by chance that it had rolled near the boat, perhaps driven by the waves of the Kinneret.

Someone who is responsible for all the time-pieces on the coast of the Sea of Galilee simply pulled the switch and stopped time. The tireless excavators continued working with devotion, with emotion and with caution. When almost a meter of the other strake had already been exposed, Moshe suddenly called out, "Here's the second plank," and out of the darkness, like the angel of God, Orna Cohen hopped in quickly and supported the second plank, which suddenly started to bend inward into the boat's internal space, which had previously been

Work continued at night under fishermen's lights

filled with the silt and mud that had hardened together and supported the boat's sides. Now that the mud had been removed from the inside to the outside of the boat, an empty space had been created in the boat and, were it not for Orna's intuitive and swift reaction the entire second plank would have collapsed or bent inwards.

But light-footed Orna, with a long, strong, stable metal rod in her hands, jumped into the space inside the boat, and supported the second plank, which straightened and settled in place, and the boat was just fine.

Sudden motion could have caused the boat's frame to bend inwards, to change angle or, heaven forbid, to actually collapse or change shape. The fact that some of the team were experienced fishermen, who had built many a boat out of fiberglass, was of great importance to the success of the excavation. They were able to provide swift

Overjoyed — exposing the boat

and reliable solutions, even at night, when they were tired almost to death.

Moshe, Yuval, Orna and the other excavators realized that when the mud was removed from the inside of the boat, fiberglass reinforcements would have to be inserted in the spaces between the ribs that made up the boat's frame. And so, the excavation went on under pressure, a devoted team working round the clock, all hours of the day and night.

Chapter Six

The Revelation

Moshe recalls how, at the very beginning of the dig, when his fingers first encountered the boat's wooden ribs, he felt immediately that, although they looked as if they were quite firm, those wooden planks were completely waterlogged and were unable to bear even their own weight.

Conservation of the boat brought together a large number of problems, all of which needed a solution and quickly. Obviously, it was necessary to prevent the escape of water which had accumulated in the internal spaces of the wood, so that it would not collapse inward and crumble away. The wooden beams had to remain damp and not dry out, so water was constantly sprayed over them; a special team erected a giant tent that covered the entire dig in order to protect it from the sun. Because it was obvious that the project had to be carried out in the shortest possible time, electricity generators and fishermen's lamps were brought

in to light up the night. The workers were divided into daytime groups and nighttime groups and the excavation was conducted around the clock with no breaks, continuing for twelve consecutive days and nights and one more night.

The heavy layer of mud and silt that had adhered to every inch of the boat's frame had protected it for two thousand years, but it was still evident to all the excavators that, in clearing it away, they were carrying out a labor of love. Scaffolding was erected for the workers and they lay on platforms and cleared away the sticky mud with their hands, carefully and with infinite love.

Clearing out the mud from the boat's interior meant that the space it left had to be replaced, gradually, with fiberglass. Fiberglass is a material that is made up of several components. The process of manufacturing fiberglass is called pultrusion because of its fabrication process, which involves pulling a collection of glass fibers through a resin bath and then through a heated die to cure the resin. Fiberglass is irreversible; it cannot be reformed or melted like PVC. Sometimes plastic tubes are introduced to the process, to give flexibility to the material and make it easy to shape into the necessary angle, for example for filling the spaces between a boat's ribs. The temperature and humidity influence the speed at which the fiberglass sets and this can take place over a few minutes or up to an hour and a half.

The fiberglass, custom molded as the team excavated the boat and passed over the boat's side into its inner space toward the inner ribs by way of a circumferential hoop, indeed prevented the inward collapse of the boat's wooden ribs.

It was not only the boat's inner space that had to be protected; its outside had to be taken care of, too. And thus, the excavators dug ditches alongside and close to the boat's wooden frame, right down to its base. Each ditch was wide enough to hold a man and it was a strange sight indeed, to see a grown man lying on his back or on his side digging away with such joy as to be totally oblivious of the fact that his body was immersed in mud.

The diggers lay on both sides of the boat, in the man-made ditches, deep in wet mud, digging down toward the boat's base. Full of excitement, they anticipated the moment at which one of them would meet the person on the other side, who was equally anxious to be the first one to meet someone from the other side. And thus they worked around the clock, around the boat, and a benign spirit surrounded the workers' camp, around and around, watching over them.

Even at the very beginning, when the excavators' fingers touched the boat's wooden ribs, they could feel how they were waterlogged, which made them very soft. They had to be handled with the greatest of care. And the level of concern rose: how was it going to be possible to transfer the boat — a long lump, 8.20 meters long and 2.30 meters wide. So large, yet as soft as butter.

Telephone calls went out in all directions: to Israel's naval commanders, and air force commanders, to the management of the nuclear reactor and to companies that owned giant cranes.

Yuval suddenly recalled the *Vasa*. The royal Swedish warship *Vasa* capsized in the Baltic Sea on her maiden voyage in August 1628 and never once fired her guns at the enemy. Raised in 1961, the *Vasa* is the only well-preserved seventeenth-century warship in the world. Three hundred thirty years the Vasa spent deep under water until it was recovered. But research has shown that the ancient Kinneret boat and the *Vasa* have nothing in common and no comparisons can be made.

These are the reasons why the *Vasa* was in pretty good condition after 333 years underwater:

(1) The ship was brand new at the time of sinking

(2) Salinity in the Baltic Sea is 0.4 percent and shipworms do not thrive

(3) The water surrounding the *Vasa* contained no oxygen

(4) Neither ice nor currents had caused any damage

(5) The water temperature remained steady between 1 and 5 degrees C (33.8–41 degrees F)

(6) The ship was built chiefly of oak heartwood with a high iron content.

The Scandinavian people are traditionally seafaring people and were well versed in working the various kinds of metal. They heated, cut and rolled the molten metal and knew exactly how to create excellent alloy from it. Thus, the *Vasa* sunk to the depths and remained there for only 333 years preserved intact, and there were no special problems involved in bringing it back onto dry land without causing it any harm.

It soon became very clear to the Kinneret boat excavation team that they could learn nothing from the *Vasa* on how to transfer the ancient boat from the Sea of Galilee.

And the excavation went on and the concerns creased the foreheads of the workers and they

Coating the boat in polyurethane foam

continued to send telegrams to all parts of the globe, while telephone conversations, advice and the wheels of thought continued to turn inside their heads. The team came up with a new proposal: to dismantle the boat and to mark each part with a serial number, to keep the parts in containers, and later, to put it all together again

The construction of a row of external polyurethane foam supports facilitated clearance of the remaining mud beneath the hull

poultry suffered from the terribly high summer temperatures inside their coops, he had been searching for some kind of material that would insulate roofs against the summer heat. Moshe discovered polyurethane foam. When two kinds of material are sprayed in foam form on top of one another, a reaction occurs, the temperatures rise, the material expands, air pockets form inside it and when the new material cools

according to the serial numbers. Moshe, who had felt with his fingertips how sodden the boat's wood was and how thin, was quite certain that once the boat was dismantled into small pieces, it would never be possible to put it together again.

Moshe walked around, worried, and went to visit the chickens — at that time he was working in the kibbutz poultry farms — and it was here that he remembered how, in the summer, when he noticed how badly the

The boat covered inside and out with polyurethane foam

down and hardens, it becomes insulating material. And thus, when they sprayed the two types of material on the chicken roof, what they got was a polyurethane-covered chicken coop.

The advantages of polyurethane were obvious. It's hard, so it would provide support for the boat's skeleton from inside and out. They knew another important fact: when the polyurethane cools, it expands, its specific weight drops and it can float on water. When Moshe mentioned polyurethane to Orna, her eyes opened wide in alarm. She was afraid the meeting of two highly combustible materials would harm the waterlogged wood. And then Moshe suggested, "Orna, why don't you at least try spraying some of the two materials onto a tiny part of the boat's wood — don't do it straight onto the wood, which is very tender and vulnerable, but onto a plastic sheet closely covering the wood — and see what happens…" Before Moshe had even finished

his sentence, Orna was already off to try out the idea.

Rotem, a fellow "digger," who was standing close to the two, heard the word "polyurethane," jumped up suddenly and went over to them. "Just

At last the whole boat was covered beneath and above

a moment," he said, "you said polyurethane, didn't you? I've got someone for you who's an expert in polyurethane." And Moshe turned to Rotem, smiling his good smile. "Let's just wait a minute," he said, "let's just see what Orna says." And this might be the right place to describe Moshe's very special smile, which spreads all over his face and has the power to melt hearts. And then Moshe went to Orna, who was standing and examining the effect of the material on a tiny piece of the boat.

The experiment was successful and Moshe didn't have to ask Orna anything. When he looked into her eyes, he saw the double rainbow that had lit up the skies for him on that day that the boat was discovered, and here, suddenly, that same rainbow lit up Orna's eyes.

In fact, Moshe and Orna saw, already as the excavation was underway, how the boat would sail once again after two thousand years.

Chapter Seven

Scientific Verification

The paths leading to the excavation were crowded with people: neighbors, relatives, people from neighboring kibbutzim, from moshavim near the Sea of Galilee, people flowing in from afar, as far afield even as the Negev.

Archaeologists, laymen, and even tourists who happened to be in the Holy Land: the big bird in the sky had led them all here. In the Holy Land, as everyone knows, rumors have wings.

And now, in the footsteps of all the other visitors, there was a sudden visit by Mr. Thomas Pickering, US Ambassador to Israel. He looked at the dig, bent over to get a better view, looked at the excavators, returned to examine the boat, listened to Moshe and Yuval's descriptions, then exchanged some words with Professor Shelley Wachsmann and Dr. Kurt Raveh and lost nothing of his excitement. It was clear to everyone that deep inside many of the people who were flowing in to see the boat, there lay hidden amateur archaeologists. In the ambassador, the boat found a real friend.

In fact, all the US embassy staff pitched in to help the excavation project in every way possible: in fundraising, in searching for information and, especially, in bringing over the world expert in ancient boats, Dr. J. Richard Steffy, from the Institute of Nautical Archaeology, Texas A&M University, who was contacted and agreed to study the boat. This meant that the hull had to be visible by the time he arrived.

The professor, who was infected like all the others with the general excitement, set off immediately for the Holy Land.

Moshe and Yuval, and even Shelley and Kurt, were awed. "He is the biggest authority of all," Moshe and Yuval whispered through dry lips, "and we are so small." And not only did no one dare to talk, they hardly dared even to breathe.

When Professor Steffy arrived he found the

excavators huddled close to the boat. And they all felt a wondrous gust of wind blow out of the boat and penetrate their bodies, flowing through their veins and infusing them with confidence, and, trembling, they raised their eyes. The professor appeared to them so tall.

His face wore a serious expression. He looked at the boat, bent down, touched it, bent anew and touched some more. He examined, advanced, measured, and no one could believe that the professor was barely able to speak.

Finally he began to talk: "The mortise and tenon system, according to which the boards are joined, informs us that this is an ancient boat. This method was used in boats that were built in the Mediterranean from the second century BCE at least until the Roman era. Moreover, anyone who knows anything about shipbuilding can see that this is an ancient boat. These days, shipbuilders first construct the frame and only later do they nail on the outer boards. In olden days, they built boats in the opposite order; in other words, first

they built the outside boards and later inserted the frame.

"If you send a tiny fragment of the wood, you'll be able to date the time at which the tree was felled." And, indeed, a fragment of the wood was sent for carbon dating and the confirmation soon came, to the effect that the tree had been felled between the first century BCE and the first century CE.

Professor Steffy passed his glance over all the excavators, stopped at Moshe's shining face and

Now the boat was ready to be transferred

Yuval's glowing eyes and went on: "This is an ancient boat that was built especially for sailing on an inter-continental body of water — the Sea of Galilee. In a seafaring boat, the outer boards are between 7 and 10 centimeters (2.8 and 3.9 in.) thick. This boat, which was built for use in the Sea of Galilee, has outer boards that are 2 centimeters (0.8 in.) wide only." And he bent down once again, scrutinized the nails, took in the whole of the exposed part of the boat and asked, "Can you hear the story of the boat?"

"The first person who worked on the boat was a master boat-wright. I guess he planned to build a beautiful vessel for his own use. His hands came out of his heart. But something happened to him — maybe he lost his money and was forced to

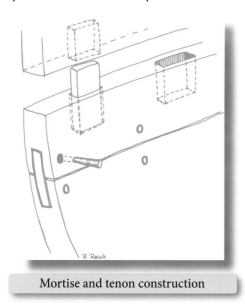

Mortise and tenon construction

sell the boat to another builder. The second boat-wright was probably less skilled than the first, maybe he was a carpenter and not a boat-wright. Look for yourselves, how many nails he used. See the number of nails he knocked in, in all kinds of angles. The nails tell a story.

"Because the second boat-wright was not as certain of his ability to build a boat and feared that he might not have joined the planks with enough nails, he feared that the boat might come apart the moment she started to sail on water. To be on the safe side, therefore, he exaggerated with his use of nails.

"But if you take a look at the nails you'll see that two thousand years ago they already knew how to manufacture nails of excellent quality. It's a fact: every nail that didn't protrude above the level of the wood did not rust for over two thousand years." And the professor straightened and looked into the eyes of all the excavators, saw the stars that had begun to shine in them and said: "This is a most fascinating and valuable discovery. Please allow me to share your excitement."

Professor Steffy confirmed the boat's age and was happy that the excavators were digging it out with the suitable measure of care, and that they made a point of confirming the correct action to take whenever necessary. And thus, infused with happiness and pride, they all sat down close to the boat and looked at each other and sailed off on a sea of memories.

19. RADIOCARBON DATING OF THE BOAT

ISRAEL CARMI

The ^{14}C method was applied to date wood used in the construction of the Kinneret boat. Ten samples from the hull as well as two samples from wood fragments found nearby were analyzed, as presented in Table 1.

In the analysis, the residual activity of the samples was measured in proportional counters (Carmi, Noter and Schlesinger 1971; Carmi 1987). After correcting the residual activity for possible changes affected in its isotopic composition by chemical processes, the conventional ^{14}C age of the sample (using the 5570 year half-life) was calculated, and then calibrated (Stuiver and Pearson 1986), in order to provide the calendaric ages presented in Table 1.

Table I
Ages of Samples from the Kinneret Boat and
of Related Timber Determined by the ^{14}C Method

Sample	Part	No.	Type	^{14}C age		Calendaric age
RT767A	Strake			1940 ± 100	BP	40 CE
RT767B	Frame			2080 ± 90	BP	100 BCE
RT772A	Strake	6		2140 ± 100	BP	130 BCE
RT772B	Frame	42A		1900 ± 100	BP	80 CE
RT773A	Fragment of					
	Assembly 1			1930 ± 100	BP	70 CE
RT793A	Frame	78	*Quercus*	1960 ± 130	BP	40 CE
RT793B	Strake	24	*Cedrus*	2000 ± 100	BP	0 CE
RT793C	Strake	62	*Cedrus*	2110 ± 110	BP	120 BCE
RT794D	Assembly 3					
	beneath boat	A657/2		2030 ± 110	BP	40 BCE
RT794E	Strake	A61/14		2100 ± 120	BP	100 BCE
RT794F	Strake	46		2060 ± 120	BP	90 BCE
RT794G	Tenon					
	from strake	10		1960 ± 110	BP	40 CE

The carbon dating and the confirmation of the time one of the trees used in the boat's construction had been felled — between the last century BCE and the first century CE

Chapter Eight

Sailing Away on a Memory

Kurt closed his eyes so tightly that his eyelids almost got stuck together. Then he opened his eyes, pondered for a moment and said: "I can recall that day at dawn when the excavations began for this boat, when we went out and suddenly saw the Migdalites digging with a dumper and tractors, and the excavators were surrounded by a threatening chain of riflemen, all from Migdal. And Moshe and Yuval stepped forward, rubbing their eyes in disbelief that those same Migdalites, with whom they had grown up, were suddenly pretending not to know them, as if they had never seen them.

"In the meantime," Kurt went on, "I raised my eyes to the skies and couldn't believe what I saw: there, at the edges of the sky, a storm wind had gathered up a large group of black, angry clouds, swollen with water, threatening to open up and pour their waters over the Sea of Galilee. And the wind continued to collect those dark clouds,

storming over the Sea of Galilee, whipping up the waves that had started to chase one another in fury. And," Kurt went on, "I tried to breathe as deeply as I could, to take in air, to really fill my lungs to their utmost capacity, but I wasn't able to. And before I had even understood and taken in the entire picture, I could hear the loud sounds of rolling thunder.

"The Sea of Galilee Administration people had appeared, driving up on their heavy-duty vehicles and, in the most amazing speed, tempered with excitement and energy, their entire team set about building a dyke all around the spot at which the boat was found. And the dyke was tall and firm and strong and the *Sharqiya*, which had already arrived at the dyke, took fright and dropped, terrified, at its feet." And Kurt went on, "And Avi Eitan, who heads the Department of Antiquities, looked around him, took in the threatening wind blowing in from the Migdalites, and, with a speed that is unprecedented in the world of archaeology, declared that the whole area was a 'closed' archaeological site.

"To this day, I don't understand and can't fathom how it was possible for such an operation, which involved the recruitment of so many people, and money, and equipment and machines, and licenses and permits and supplies, all of which would normally have taken at least a year to organize, was underway — unbelievably — in less than an hour.

"Please recall, ladies and gentlemen, how we started off, a mere four people with two hoes and a miserable jeep, with hardly any equipment, without any permits and without any money at all, and, in fact, it looked as if everything was against us. Conditions were terrible, and we were all under awful pressure and in a mad race against time and against the Migdalites and the winds in the skies and the powers of nature and here, a regular miracle happened and within just one hour — the dig had begun."

And, inside his mind, Kurt traveled back in time, to the days of his childhood, and he continued to tell his audience: "I grew up in a Christian family and throughout my childhood I was taught the stories of the New Testament and when I listened to those stories, I imagined them in terms of colorful pictures which described to me the stories of the Bible. And the pictures that were inside my head have stayed with me all the

days of my life. When I came to the Holy Land, I of course went first to visit all the places that are mentioned in the New Testament and wherever I went, none of the places resembled the descriptions that I saw in my mind's eye, but, when I came to the Kinneret — I was amazed!

"It was early in the morning. I sat down here on the shore of the Kinneret and the sun, as it rose, colored the whole sky with red and for the first time, I saw the real picture that had been in my mind and that had accompanied me throughout my childhood: the red sunrise over the Kinneret. I felt myself being drawn into the pastoral scenery, and I breathed in the silence that blew over me from the Kinneret. I sat there and didn't even feel the time passing and suddenly I understood why, in every basilica and in every church that I had ever visited, I always saw a drawing or a mosaic of the Kinneret. And on the sea, there is always a boat, in which Jesus sat with the fishermen," Kurt went on. "This boat and its occupants have sunk deep down into my soul."

And all the excavators sat around the boat, spellbound and speechless by the story that Dr. Kurt Raveh told them. A light breeze blew in from the boat, a special spirit, the spirit of generosity, the spirit of boundless giving, and it spread in all directions and was drawn into all the people there. Moshe and Yuval sensed it, perhaps even more than the other people present, and Moshe straightened, looked at Yuval and Kurt and Shel-

Ancient anchors discovered around the Sea of Galilee

ley and said: "It seems to me that this spirit is promising us that this boat will bring peace. And here, from this boat, peace will return to the world and to all peoples."

And Dr. Kurt Raveh, who grew up in a Chris-

tian home in Holland and loved to listen to the voice of his father — who fired his imagination with stories from the Bible — glanced at the exposed hull of the boat, at the people sitting together as if stuck to each other, looked at the

Kinneret which was sending its waves toward them and said: "Two thousand years ago, a man came to this place and wandered all around the Kinneret. He approached the people who lived here and all the cripples and the lepers whom everyone avoided and who were so neglected in their misery, and he approached them and comforted them and encouraged them and wiped away their tears and tried to heal them and went to the fishermen and talked to them in their fishing boats.

"He was drawn into the peace and the quiet that dwelt here with the people and swallowed with his eyes the wide spaces of the horizon. He collected in his heart the blue of the Kinneret and the green of the landscapes along the coasts, talked with everyone and asked to help them all. And all he wanted was to break down the wall of hatred between one man and another and to teach love and that is why I think, like Moshe, that this boat, at the end of the day, will bring peace!"

Chapter Nine

The Boat Sails Again

The years from 1983 to 1986 were dry years and the water level of the Sea of Galilee had gone down by three whole meters. The Kinneret had run away from its coast. But, just as the excavation to retrieve the boat began, the rains came. The sea began filling up quickly and made its way toward the treasure. The waves churned and the hearts of the excavators churned in fear. But this fear only increased the volunteering spirit of the people of Kibbutz Ginosar and, for every excavator who took time off to rest, there flowed in new people eager to join the excavation project.

The task now was to move the boat to a conservation tank where the fragile wood could be strengthened. Orna, the country's only expert on boat conservation, working alone and without precedent, had to be open to innovative and creative solutions. Having decided on Moshe's combined polyurethane insulation method, she determined together with Moshe and Yuval that the boat would be covered in polyurethane foam late at night, by a small group of volunteer excavators and in the absence of nosy onlookers.

And so, late one night, after midnight, Eli quietly drove up in a van, out of which he rolled barrels containing polyurethane. Kurt and Shelley covered a tiny portion of the boat's hull with a sheet of polyethylene and polyurethane foam was sprayed over it, at first a millimeter-thick layer, which expanded immediately to 1 centimeter (0.4 in.), and then hardened. Covering the boat with polyurethane foam was a huge success and this success made the people happy and they continued covering the hull with polyethylene sheets and more foam and so on and so forth until, without their even noticing it, the dawn had arrived.

The new day spread its wings on the world and the team responsible for covering the boat with polyurethane foam continued with their task all that day and into the night and then came the second dawn. By the end of the second day the entire body of the boat was covered in expanded polyurethane foam and the boat's body was no longer visible; in its stead had grown a huge lump of polyurethane that did not reveal what was inside it. Moshe said to Yuval, "That's it, she's ready for her journey!"

Moshe and Yuval and Kurt and Shelley looked at each other and Kurt asked if they remembered when they had been so vulnerable (right after the boat was discovered), and might even have gone astray, how all those institutions that usually are only good at complicating matters had instead, when the boat was involved, always been there to help. The Sea Authority (now known as the Sea of Galilee Authority) and the National Water Carrier (Mekorot) and the Department of Antiquities (now the Israel Antiquities Authority), all those people and all their equipment, only had to hear that the ancient boat project — which, by then, was already coined the "Jesus boat" — was stuck and immediately all those institutions linked arms and set off to help.

Now all that vast crowd that gathered on the beach looked on with anxious eyes at the lump of polyurethane and suddenly, above the storm of waves rose the sound of all the heavy equipment. The spreading commotion increased and to Yuval and to Moshe and to all the great crowd that had gathered there it sounded like the wonderful melody of angels and here they are a-coming.

It was the tractors and the dumpers and the bulldozers and the cranes: all the equipment that had previously been used to dig ditches. The largest dozer, which only a few months before had itself built the dam, now opened its giant jaws and the dam collapsed and split. And those pumps that had worked energetically at drawing out the waters were now working the other way around, starting to draw the water inwards.

The rumor about the intention to float the boat after two thousand years had resulted in columns of neighbors and friends and relatives, members of the press and the merely curious — even kindergarten children were all arriving as if from nowhere.

So many pairs of feet. At first, people gathered around the pit in which lay the giant polyurethane lump. Then the numbers of people grew, until there was no longer any room around the pit. And because of the crowded conditions, masses of people started dispersing along the beach. They all wanted to see the boat floating. All eyes were fixed on the pit. And suddenly, before everyone's eyes, the polyurethane lump peeped up at the spectators.

The excitement grew. The water continued to rise inside the pit and the lump continued to rise with the water level. And the huge crowd held its breath and fell silent while at the edge of the world only the sounds made by the large pumps and the heavy equipment could be heard. The unbelievable was happening: the boat began to move and floated out onto the water. People's throats choked up and no one managed to utter a word.

Then someone started clapping his hands and the entire crowd was carried away with emotion and joined in, cheering and clapping. Moshe and Yuval looked at Orna, who wiped away a tear but was unable to say a word, and Moshe said: "This boat is a living creature with a will of its own and either it, or Someone up there above us all, has determined the order of things and the timetable."

And the boat set off on its journey, floating on the Sea of Galilee. With timing

Water was pumped back into the excavation pit; a steam shovel dug a channel in the sea and the boat was floated out to the lake

so accurate as to be supernatural, the kibbutz's twelfth-graders arrived, having just returned from a marine science lesson with a large rowboat, and, as if it were the most natural thing in the world and every afternoon they encounter such a boat, they undertook the job of leading the boat to the fishing pier at Kibbutz Ginosar. And maybe it was some hidden hand that led things thus, with the actual intention of leading the boat back home, after two thousand years.

Orna, overcome with excitement, burst forward, hopped over the waves after the boat, caught up with it, jumped aboard and sat down, as if all her life she had been riding on boats. And Moshe watched the boat and its rider and was suddenly gripped by a feeling he had never known before and which troubles him to this day. Why did he and Yuval not storm the boat, too — why did they not also jump on the boat in order to sit on it on its maiden voyage after two thousand years?

And Moshe thought: true, many people volunteered, with joy and heartfelt love, but, maybe, this boat is just a tiny bit theirs, just a little, just a little more than anyone else's…

The boat sails once more in the Sea of Galilee

Preparing the Conservation Pool

The boat was floated into the fishing pier at Kibbutz Ginosar and, for one night, it had returned to anchor among fishing boats.

Even before the transfer to the fishing pier, Orna handed out clear instructions as to the building of the pool in which the boat was to be preserved, including detailed requirements regarding the equipment to be used for tempering and the conditions in which the boat was to be completely immersed, with controls, equipment for heating the solution in the tank and a mechanism for circulating it, a gauge for humidity, etc., the main principle being that the pool had to be as small as possible in order to lose the least possible amount of energy. The inside of the pool had to be lined with substances that would not be damaged by the conservation chemicals. Orna had decided to give the pool a double ceramic

The ancient boat was moored alongside the modern boats in the harbor of Kibbutz Ginosar

A crane places the boat in a conservation tank for the next 14 years

lining, smoothing down one layer, pressing it down and then applying another layer, and pressing it down again.

And thus, while one group was constructing the conservation pool, a second group appropriated a crane. An apparatus was prepared for raising the boat, the crane arrived, steel cables were stretched and the boat was lifted up and then lowered onto a raised surface between the Yigal Allon Center and the conservation pool, which was still in the process of being built.

With a sense of holy mission, the two groups carried out their work. One group took care of the boat's keel, carefully and accurately removing the remains of the expanded polyurethane, while constantly making sure to keep wetting the wooden keel, so that, heaven forbid, the two-thousand-year-old water should not "slip away" from the spaces in the boards. Because then, the worst of all would happen and the wooden boards would dry out and become distorted, disintegrate and, heaven forbid, the boat would turn into dust.

In the meantime, the construction of the conservation pool was completed. Now, a crane was ordered once again, once again the steel cables were stretched, the crane lifted up the boat and all those involved froze as the crane that raised the boat began to shake and the boat with it! Again, the team exhibited initiative and agility that is out of this world. A number of pairs of hands grabbed at the boat, a number of pairs of hands grabbed at the crane and in no time at all they had stabilized it and then, when they looked carefully, it was apparent that the whole operation had almost failed because they had not placed the crane on a flat surface. But the God of all the boats took care of the boat's keel.

Again they organized themselves; this time they used all their eyes — those in their heads and those in their hearts — to make sure that the crane was placed firmly on the ground. And then the boat was immersed in the conservation pool.

Usually, when a boat is raised

The boat in its conservation pool

from the bottom of a salty sea, it is necessary to wait about four years before it becomes possible to begin the process of conservation. In the case of this boat, it was possible after two years, because the Sea of Galilee is a sweet-water lake.

But even during those two years of waiting for the preservation solution (the boat was immersed only in water for the first two years), there was a lot of work still to do. It was necessary to build giant heating apparatuses, each two meters high, instruments for measuring humidity and heat, instruments for tempering and conditioning and for circulating the solution in the pool.

In addition to all these, a structure had to be built in which to house the conservation pool; it was twelve meters long and five meters wide (40×16 ft.). And since the structure was locked, one of the walls was built entirely of glass, so that the boat's admirers could take an occasional peep at it.

Chapter Eleven

The Miracle of Moshe and the St. Peter's Fish

"One morning," Moshe recalled, "Orna came to me, pale and breathless, and literally dropped down beside me. Orna was barely able to utter a few words," Moshe continued, "and I was barely able to put together a single coherent sentence, until I managed to understand what Orna was saying. That same morning when she had gone to see the boat, Orna discovered to her horror that live worms were swimming happily around the boat's wooden keel. Orna was filled with the fear of God — that the worms would damage the boat."

She went to Moshe scared to death. And Moshe, with amazing cool, suggested the kind of solution that only a second-generation fisherman could come up with. At first he tried to reassure Orna, and then he said to her: "Orna, I'm going to my father, Yanky, and I'll get a bucket of St. Peter's Fish and some goldfish and drop them into the pool with the boat."

When Moshe returned with the St. Peter's Fish and the goldfish, Orna was sitting next to the conservation pool, looking extremely worried.

Moshe poured the fish into the pool. Orna watched the fish swimming around the boat and couldn't believe her eyes. Slowly, all the worms in the pool disappeared, the ferns disappeared, the seaweed disappeared and the water was clear — the miracle of Moshe and the St. Peter's Fish, God bless them!

Moshe looked at the boat's wooden keel, then at the fish and, again, at Orna; now, at last some of the color was gradually seeping back into her cheeks.

Only half an hour ago Orna had believed that the skies had fallen in on her head and the boat which, for her, was the archaeological find of the twentieth century at least, was suddenly in danger of devastation. And then Moshe, a second-generation fisherman, with maturity of soul and endless initiative, came up with an idea that was amazing in its simplicity — and saved the boat.

Orna looked at Moshe and looked at the fish and couldn't get enough of the sight, and suddenly, as if out of a dream, she heard Moshe telling her what he had heard from his father and from Mendel Nun.

Today, the waves of the Sea of Galilee are cut by fish from Africa, Asia and the north. Alongside all the newcomers, the sea is shared by fish which are indigenous to the region and all the various species swim together in the sea, each of them according to the habits of its ancestors in its land of origin.

Many species of the St. Peter's Fish, also called tilapia (or Amnon) came over from tropical Africa and so did the catfish. Schools of carps, which originated in India, sought waterways through to the Sea of Galilee and species of fish even made their way from the far north.

Of the various species of fish of the carp family whose origin is in India, only one survived and is identical to those in India. All the remaining species of carp here are endemic to the Land of Israel. The catfish also came to the region, and now swims in the River Nile.

Moshe, for whom the world of the fish is so familiar, explained to Orna about the habitat of her new favorite fish: "The Sea of Galilee is a truly special lake. Josephus Flavius wrote nineteen hundred years ago that the types of fish in the region of the Nile are different in taste and in appearance from the fish in any other place. He knew that both in the Nile River in Egypt and in the Sea of Galilee in the Land of Israel, the same catfish can be found, and from this simple fact, Josephus Flavius tried to assume that there might even be an underground connection between the Nile and the Sea of Galilee.

"The uniqueness of the Sea of Galilee," Moshe told Orna, "is in the variety of fish that swim in it. It has fish from the north, from the south, from the east and they are all here together in the Sea of Galilee and continue to follow the same lifestyle that characterizes the members of their species in their countries of origin. Fishermen are usually forbidden to catch fish during the egg-laying season, but in the Sea of Galilee, which is home to so many different kinds of fish, each variety has its own separate egg-laying season, which is different from that of the egg-laying periods of the other species. The egg-laying season of the entire fish population extends from early winter all the way to the end of summer.

"And this fact does not benefit the fish, because it leaves no possibility to hold a season during which it is forbidden to catch fish due to the egg-laying season."

Orna watched the fish swimming around the boat, and Moshe saw her affection for them, so he went on: "My father, too, loved the St. Peter's Fish better than all the others. In winter, when the sea

The Sea of Galilee (Photo: Arie Erlich. EdcomGlobal)

water became very cold, he would wrap himself up in a blanket, and he feared that the St. Peter's Fish might also have been cold, because they are a species of fish that comes from the tropical regions. Father would row his boat, following the St. Peter's Fish, and they 'drew' paths for him on the water and led him to the warm springs near Tabha where they would spend the winter months.

"Sometimes Father forgot to catch fish and would spend his time observing the lives and habits of the St. Peter's Fish. And it was then that he discovered that in late April every year, adult St. Peter's Fish would pair up and start 'going steady.' Each couple chooses its own territory and the male chases away any alien St. Peter's Fish who dares invade his territory. Mrs. St. Peter's Fish very nearly wrinkles her brow at the sight

of her partner chasing off the stranger, until she understands that her partner fights fiercely for his home. He stiffens his fins, opens his air ducts wide, and his rigid body floats alongside the invader.

"Mrs. St. Peter's Fish thinks to herself, of all the St. Peter's Fish in the sea, my own St. Peter's Fish is the one most worthy of becoming the father of my offspring, because according to game theory, a female is wise if she chooses the most successful male to father her brood, in order to give them the best chance of survival.

"And Mr. St. Peter's Fish, who knows how to read his wife's mind, hurries off to dig a cavity in the sand, and his lady partner dives down and pushes the walls of the cavity aside and he dives in from the other side to deepen the cavity, and she reappears, only this time, she slips straight down and lays her eggs and the male swims down and fertilizes the eggs and they continue with this bridal dance until the cavity is filled up with a sticky mass of eggs and then the two fish open their mouths as wide as they can, and completely fill them with fertilized eggs.

"For fourteen days and fourteen nights the fish will eat nothing, and will only pass fresh water through their jaws in order to supply the eggs with oxygen. Two weeks after the eggs are laid, the two adult fish open their jaws wide and the tiny fish swim out. For the first time, the little fish get to meet their parents and the Sea of Galilee. It is very exciting to see how the St. Peter's Fish lead and maneuver their little ones, taking them to hiding places and to places where there is plenty of food for them to feed on. And if the little fishes are in sudden danger, the parent fish immediately open their jaws wide and all the little ones burst into their mouths. The parent fishes' mouths are actually a place of shelter and security for the little baby fish."

Orna listened intently, looking at the fish, scrutinizing the boat inside the pool's now-clear water, marveling at the miracle that took place literally before her very eyes, and she said: "Moshe, I shall never, ever harm a fish that is going steady with another St. Peter's Fish. It is as near to being human as can be."

Chapter Twelve

Twelve Kinds of Trees Make Up a Boat

Trees have always captured the imagination of human beings. Many legends have been spun about trees and grew together with the trees. Trees grow roots deep into the earth and grow high up to the heavens. Some trees grow tall and others are hundreds of years old, and man has learned to relate to the trees and to the forest in which they grow as nature's medicine store, like a modern-day pharmacy. Dr. Ella Werker, of the Department of Botany at the Hebrew University of Jerusalem, analyzed the wood of which the ancient boat was built and discovered that it is made of the wood of twelve different trees, all indigenous to the area of the Sea of Galilee:

- Sidder or Christ's Thorn Jujube — *Ziziphus spina-christi*
- Carob — *Ceratonia siliqua*
- Aleppo pine — *Pinus halepensis*
- Spiny hawthorn — *Crataegus aronia*
- Cedar of Lebanon — *Cedrus libani*
- Tabor oak — *Quercus ithaburensis*
- Common wllow — *Salix acmophylla*
- Laurel — *Laurus nobilis*
- Redbud (Judas tree) — *Cercis siliquastrum*
- Sycamore fig — *Ficus sycomorus*
- Atlantic terebinth — *Pistacia atlantica*
- Oriental plane tree — *Platanus orientalis*

The tree that provided most of the boat's timber is the Cedar of Lebanon. This is a tree that is unusually strong and hardy. King Solomon, who was aware of the strength and quality of this wood, had it imported especially from Lebanon, for use in building the Temple in Jerusalem. In olden days, just as gold was considered a precious metal, so, too, was the Cedar of Lebanon considered precious among the trees. The Cedar of Lebanon is less destructible than other trees; parasites are less likely to attack it because they don't like the

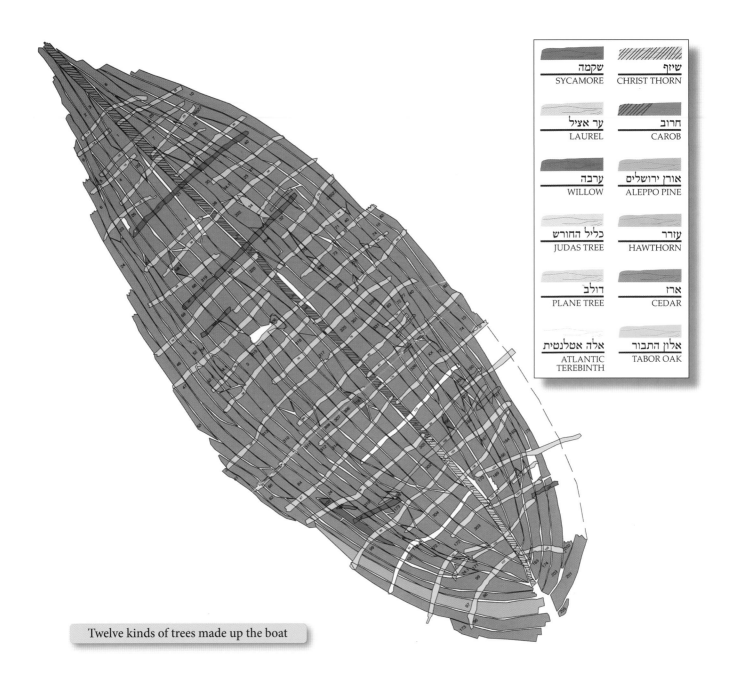

שיזף	CHRIST THORN	שקמה	SYCAMORE
חרוב	CAROB	ער אציל	LAUREL
אורן ירושלים	ALEPPO PINE	ערבה	WILLOW
עזרר	HAWTHORN	כליל החורש	JUDAS TREE
ארז	CEDAR	דולב	PLANE TREE
אלון התבור	TABOR OAK	אלה אטלנטית	ATLANTIC TEREBINTH

Twelve kinds of trees made up the boat

taste of its sap. This is a fact that the boat-wrights discovered, and they used to paint cedar sap on the wood of their boats in order to repel worms and other parasites.

The boat's frame was built of wood from the Tabor oak, a powerful, long-living tree. In the middle of the Israeli village of Pardes Hanna, there stands a large Tabor oak tree whose age has been estimated at over 250 years old. Just imagine the events that have taken place under that tree over the years of its life.

There are some interesting stories connected to the Tabor oak. The raven is a bird that likes to feed on acorns. It is also a clever bird, clever enough to know the nutritional value of acorns. So how does the oak cooperate with the raven?

It creates a bitter-tasting substance and concentrates it near the fruit, at a place in which the embryo is located from which the new acorn will eventually develop. The raven finds the acorn and flies off with it, making sure to eat only the part that is not bitter, leaving the embryo intact. Thus, the raven has food and, in return, it spreads the seed of the Tabor oak, without doing it any harm; and both parties are happy.

The willow tree, which the Arabs call "Jumis," is another type of wood in the boat. When she visited the Holy Land in the second half of the eighteenth century, the artist Mary Rogers painted an amazingly accurate picture of this wonderful, shady tree.

The boat's keel had been broken in two places and both places had been repaired (two thousand years ago) with the branches of the Domim (as it is called today by the Arabs). The tree is also known as Sidder or Christ's Thorn. According to Christian tradition, the crown of thorns placed on Jesus' head by the Roman soldiers as he made his way to the cross was made of a branch of the Sidder.

Another tree used in building the boat was the carob tree, whose roots go right down into the aquifer. It is known as a holy tree, maybe because of its longevity. It is a symbol of steadfastness and, according to tradition, the carob symbolizes stoicism. There is a story about Rabbi Shimon bar Yochai, who spoke out sharply against the Roman Empire and was therefore forced into hiding in a cave, together with his son, Rabbi Eliezer. The two hid in the cave for thirteen years and fed on the fruit of the carob tree that grew at the cave's entrance. They got their water from the spring that flowed alongside the cave. This legend shows how nourishing is the fruit of the carob tree.

There is another fascinating fact also connected to the carob tree. In each and every carob pod, whether large and plump, or even if it is small and wrinkled, the weight of all its seeds is identical. Thus, our forebears used these seeds as a gauge for weighing gold, and each carob seed is known as a karat.

עזרר קוצני
Spiny hawthorn
Crataegus aronia

שקמה
Sycamore fig
Ficus sycomorus

חרוב מצוי
Carob
Ceratonia siliqua

שיזף מצוי
Sidder or Christ's Thorn Jujube
Ziziphus spina-christi

ערבה מחודדת
Common willow
Salix acmophylla

אלה אטלטית
Atlantic terebinth
Pistacia atlantica

אלון התבור
Tabor oak
Quercus ithaburensis

דולב מזרחי
Oriental plane tree
Platanus orientalis

אורן ירושלים
Aleppo pine
Pinus halepensis

כליל החורש
Redbud (Judas tree)
Cercis siliquastrum

ארז הלבנון
Cedar of Lebanon
Cedrus libani

ער אציל (דפנה)
Laurel
Laurus nobilis

According to the Bible, the terebinth tree (*Ela* in Hebrew) gives a wonderful shade. There is no doubt that the Bible refers to the local terebinth tree, because this is the only one that grows with a broad trunk and only under its leafy branches can people conduct their religious rituals. To this day, there are terebinth trees that arouse wonder and emotion because of their height; sometimes the terebinth will be accompanied by the Tabor oak and it is easy to understand why religious rituals take place in the shade of these magnificent trees.

Another tree fortunate enough to be included among the dozen trees that made up the two-thousand-year-old Kinneret boat is the noble laurel, which is also known as the bay tree, and its plaited branches are fashioned into crowns that are laid on the heads of victors.

Sometimes surprising lessons can be discovered from trees; the hawthorn is one such tree and is unique. If herds of goats and the axes of human beings refrain from attacking it, its leaves will grow large and broad and its few branches will end in a hard point. But if it is attacked by man and goats it will — quite incredibly — grow leaves that are small and thorny and look as if they have been cut. Strangely enough, even trees find effective ways to protect themselves!

The redbud is also known as the Judas tree. In the early spring months in the Land of Israel, even when its branches are still bare and exposed and before new foliage has grown, bright pinky-red clusters of flowers appear and the whole tree looks as if it is blushing in embarrassment — which might be the reason that it was given its name, after Judas Iscariot.

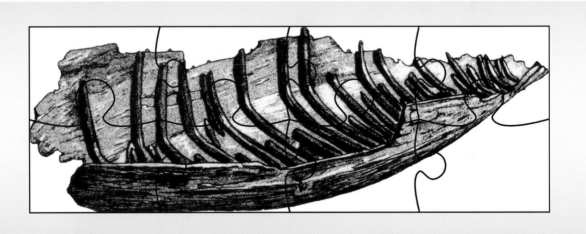

Chapter Thirteen

The Conservation —
A Labor of Love

Now it was time for the stage which appeared to be the most important of all: the conservation, a real labor of love.

Each stage of the excavation and conservation of the boat was extremely important. But at night, when everyone pondered the fate of the boat, they understood the enormity of the job of conservation.

This boat, which had spent around two thousand years in the depths of the Sea of Galilee, had soaked up enormous amounts of water. Everyone who belonged to the "Order of Boat" got goose bumps when his or her finger so much as touched the boat. Even at the touch of a hand, it was possible to sense that there were parts of the boat that — unbelievably — consisted of 90 percent water. Once the boat was removed from the Kinneret, it was going to be necessary to keep it constantly damp, because if 90 percent of the boat were to simply evaporate, the wood would turn to dust and there would be no boat!

Orna prepared a detailed, multi-stage plan for immersing the boat in conservation fluid. The first stage consisted of immersing the boat

Sixty tons of preservation fluid were donated by DOW Chemical Company USA

in a water-soluble synthetic polymer, polyethylene glycol (PEG). This would be absorbed by the waterlogged wood, eventually replacing the water in the wood cells. As it dried, it would maintain the structure of the wood cells and diminish cell collapse and shrinkage.

At first the solution was to be made up of relatively small molecules (PEG 600) which could penetrate the wood easily; PEG in this form is liquid and penetrates deeply into the molecular structure of wood. Later, a solution of larger molecules (PEG 4000) would be used; in this form PEG has a more solid, waxy structure and would penetrate wherever there were still empty spaces inside as well as coat and protect the exterior of the boat. Both forms of PEG must be kept at a high temperature or they will solidify, so the special heating elements were critical.

The boat was placed inside its sparkling new conservation pool and all the members of the "Order of the Boat" waited with it. The spirit that emanates from the boat crossed continents and oceans and arrived on the doorstep of the Dow Chemical Company in the United States of America, who, through its agents, Jacobson Agencies Ltd., was generous enough to donate the entire quantity of PEG — forty tons — necessary for conserving the boat. The PEG arrived in large, heavy containers and was stored in the cellar of the Yigal Allon Center at Kibbutz Ginosar. Everyone listened intently to Orna's instructions and took care to follow them each and every day.

Every day, the required quantity of liters was poured into the conservation pool. Orna's instructions were precise. The boat had to be fully immersed in liquid at all times; since the PEG tends to evaporate, regular proportions of PEG had to be constantly diluted into the water in the pool, kept at a constant and regular temperature, and poured into the fluid already in the pool.

Gradually, the work took on a routine. One group of workers arrived in the morning and evaluated how much PEG was missing in the conservation pool. Another group diluted the substance and added it to the pool, according to the evaluation. A blessed new calm had fallen once again on the boathouse. Orna, who from the day the boat was discovered had been connected to it with all her heart, felt suddenly as if she had been drained of all her physical and emotional strength. Exhausted, she asked Moshe if she could take a week's vacation somewhere nearby — Greece — in order to recuperate her strength. Everyone agreed that if anyone deserved a vacation, it was Orna.

But you all know Murphy's law. Orna, the boat's "guardian angel," had just taken off, and the following morning when two of the team arrived at the conservation pool, they very nearly passed out. The entire pool was fermenting.

They immediately set off at a run to Moshe,

breaking the world record in short distance sprint. And Moshe, like a tornado, made for the telephone, called Orna's parents, obtained Orna's telephone number in Greece and as soon as Moshe's voice reached Orna's ears in Greece, she immediately left Greece and arrived on the wings of an El Al plane back in Israel and to the boat's side.

Orna quickly filled a test tube with the fermenting conservation fluid and took it to the laboratory, where it was soon discovered that the conservation fluid contained sugars that were providing a good source of nourishment to various germs. But, by now, none of the "Order of the Boat" was worried. Maybe the germs who knew Orna were worried, and they had a good reason to be so. Orna introduced some chemical substance into the pool and no germ — neither fat nor thin — remained.

The days went by, but deep down in their hearts Moshe, Orna, Yuval and all the members of the "Order of the Boat" knew no peace. Someone had charged a hidden spring in each of their hearts, and every day a line of "Order of the Boat" members turned up to see how the boat was doing, immersed in its conservation pool.

One Friday, Moshe put his hand into the fluid and jumped, as if bitten by a snake. "The conservation fluid has gone cold!"

Everyone in the boat shed was gripped by horror — the stainless steel heating system had collapsed. Moshe felt around in the conservation pool and found the first heating element: it had corroded. Silence. He found a second element, and it, too, had corroded. And the third…and the fourth…and it was Friday, and everyone was pale and Rotem ventured, in a weak voice: "Maybe we should have a word with the producer of the elements. Admittedly tomorrow is Saturday, but this is a matter of life and death and an emergency does supersede even the Sabbath. And the boat is a classic example of an emergency."

And Rotem jumped up and rushed off to phone the manufacturer of the heating elements. At first, his face was grave and his voice anxious. But suddenly his face brightened up — the heating elements manufacturer would come that day!

They all worked throughout the weekend and by Monday, the new heating elements were in place and working and, again, peace reigned in the boathouse. And those who had worked without a break through Friday, Saturday, Sunday and Monday could let down their guard for a while, and no sooner were their heads on the pillow than they had sunk into a deep slumber.

Years passed…

The conservation fluid with the smaller molecules did its job over four years. Gradually, the small molecules penetrated the spaces in the boat's wood and pushed the water out. The liquid slipped in, reinforcing and stabilizing the wood, and it was now time to replace the liquid formula with a waxy one whose molecules are larger. First it was necessary to empty the pool of its preliminary conservation fluid. Everyone watched Orna and saw how tense and anxious she was. They realized that, actually, at every transition between one stage and the next, Orna was always pale and worried.

Orna was thinking about the fact that never, in any lake or sea, had attempts been made to conserve a boat that had been in sweet water for two thousand years. But the God of all the seas and the rivers helps those who are fulfilling their labor of love. And the members of the "Order of the Boat" did their best to prevent Orna from sensing their great joy, because here they were about to empty the conservation pool of its brackish water, and they would be able, once again, to take a look at the boat.

Orna had explained to them that they must place the large-molecule substance into a clean and shining container up to one-third of its depth, and then they must pour boiling water onto the grains, to melt the waxy substance. Everyone had stood around embarrassed and helpless, not knowing where they were going to find a container large enough. And how would such a container be clean and shining? And where were they going to get a supply of boiling water? And while they were still rolling

Early days in the preservation tank

their eyes in all directions, Moshe had already come up with a solution: In the orange grove, he said, he had found a container that in the distant past was used for transferring milk to the Tnuva milk factory. Not long ago, someone had polished this container and it now looked as good as new and, while Moshe was still talking, he was already out of the door.

When he returned, his face was literally glowing because he had even managed to visit the kibbutz hotel's kitchen, where he was promised a

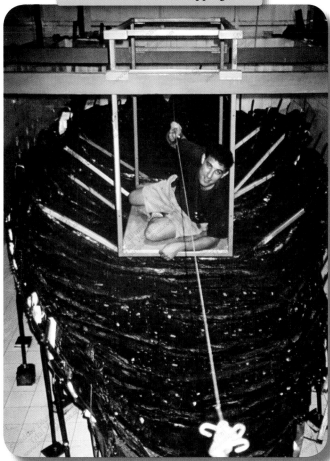

A special bridge allowed workers to treat the boat without stepping on it

supply of steam — as much as was needed. And indeed, a wonderful partnership was formed. So when the truck arrived on the big day, the first batch of conservation substance was unloaded directly off the truck and into the container, which was already hitched up to a tractor, and from there it was driven straight to the hotel kitchen, where it was filled with the exact required quantity of boiling water.

The conservation matter dissolved, and the jostling it underwent on the way back to the boathouse stirred up the formula perfectly and this was immediately poured into the conservation pool in which the boat was waiting.

The team knew that all of the second batch of conservation fluid had to be prepared, and the job could not be stopped until all of the waxy substance was dissolved. The team worked all morning and all afternoon and all evening. At midnight, the truck carrying the second conservation substance, with the larger molecules, was emptied. It was a concentrated eighteen-hour job without a break, with barely a chance to breathe, and finally the job was completed. The boat was immersed in the second conservation fluid.

Three years passed slowly. The large waxy grains completed the job of pushing the water out of the wood and replacing it with wax.

The members of the "Order of the Boat" were filled with emotion: the conservation process was completed and this time everyone was worried, and there was good reason for their concern. Imagine that something that is dearer to you than anything else is planted in your heart, you breathe it with every breath you take, and it is immersed inside a scalding hot, black, brackish liquid, and for three years you haven't seen it!

Of course everyone knew that the boat still existed and that the process had taken place. Orna had, after all, taken test tubes full of the conservation liquid to be tested, but…but…

Fear and anxiety were constantly dwelling in the hearts of those involved in saving the boat. Who knows, they thought nightmarishly, maybe the boat's sides were holding up only because the conservation fluid was quite thick and maybe as soon as the conservation fluid was removed, the boat's sides would suddenly collapse!

When the heart is gripped with fear, it seems as if the worst is about to happen.

A few days before they began emptying the conservation pool of the fluid, Moshe found yet again a very pale Orna, who begged him in a broken voice: "Moshe, don't ask!" But he, of course, immediately asked, and Orna told him her fear: "I think the boat has fallen apart!" Moshe swallowed his words and tried to say, "Why?" And Orna replied, "The shelves on which the wood samples were placed have come apart, so,

in the same way, it's quite possible that the boat has also fallen apart."

But something very strange was happening. Moshe did not appear in the least bit concerned. On the contrary! Unbelievably, he was smiling.

And then it transpired that Moshe, too, had been watching the shelves that had fallen apart. So he had stuck a broomstick into the pool to check, and felt the boat intact. Now everyone was quite certain that Someone up there was watching over them.

The members of the "Order of the Boat" came together at four in the morning, a good time to get some work done without being disturbed by tourists and curious onlookers. The level of the conservation fluid dropped gradually as it was pumped out of the pool, but the anxiety level did not drop. Suddenly, the pumps stopped working. There was fear and anxiety, and immediately a frightened telephone call to Shalom the electrician, who had already gone into retirement. Shalom arrived, repaired the fuses, called for a reduction of the pressure and work was renewed.

And the fluid level went down and everyone waited for the moment when a tiny piece of wooden board belonging to the boat would become visible. Suddenly something surfaced — but it was not a piece of boat, only a plastic tube to which one of the ribs had been attached. Then, in an instant, they could already see the top

In the conservation tank

they had prepared just in case of such an eventuality, and they attached it to the inward-bending strake, strengthening it and again, everyone let out a sigh of relief.

All that day, they worked at removing the conservation fluid that the pumps had been unable to draw out. The fluid was scalding and Rotem soaked it up with rags and he appeared not to notice! Are not Rotem's hands flesh and blood?

Rotem continued with the labor of love, not feeling the scalding fluid, not feeling the scalding rags. His hands moved and his eyes were glued to the boat. Very slowly, without anyone saying a word, everything fell silent and everyone watched the boat and here, as if out of a dream, the boat appeared in its entirety and it was as beautiful as

The end of 14 years of conservation

edge of the strake and Orna jumped up with the drawings of the boat to make sure that nothing had changed. And — O God! — the eastern edge had started to bend inward, and Yaron and Rotem rushed forward with a polystyrene plank, which

it had been, and maybe even more so. The dream had become a reality.

Except, the boat had yet to be dried, and transferred, with all possible caution, to its permanent home.

The work continued. Orna carried it out. The devotion increased. The hardships were not a deterrent. The sea of patience had not diminished. They attempted to avoid any mishap that could occur, trying to create solutions for any mishaps that might, God forbid, arise.

And all the time, their thoughts were positive, focused on arriving successfully at the final stage: the transfer of the boat to its permanent place.

They built a special bridge to make it possible to care for and clean the inside of the boat because the feeling they shared was that the boat was now much stronger and much more resilient, so that it was possible to dismantle most of the fiberglass support ribs without harming it.

The main task was defined by Orna as being that of raising the boat 20 centimeters (8 in.) off the floor.

One hundred thirty legs had been constructed; each and every leg was joined to the boat at a different angle, and made to conform exactly to the spot at which it was joined, so that each leg was of a different length.

The first problem arose — the boat was stuck along its entire bottom line to the base of the pool.

Transporting the boat to the museum

Orna heated up a thin strip of metal, which she threaded under the boat and connected, with cables and stretchers, to its sides. This job was carried out by Orna and two welders, Dotan and Jeris, and then, with endless patience, each leg, separately, was given half a turn; the boat began

The "treasure" floats in the air

Another stage was completed — wonderful.

That night Moshe dreamed about a prehistoric creature which, at any moment, would rise up and stand proudly on all its 130 legs.

Together with the pride was the enormous never-ending anxiety for the welfare of the boat. The question which troubled each of them never rose to their lips: Would they ever manage to successfully transfer the boat, intact?

Every day, Orna walked round to rise and then they began dealing with the next leg in the row, and then on to the third, and thus, with each of the 130 legs. They turned each leg a few centimeters, before moving on to the next one.

A few weeks passed and the boat stood on its metal legs, raised to a height of 20 centimeters above the floor. And the members of the "Order of the Boat" looked on it with pride, as a father would look at his baby son, standing for the first time on his own two feet.

The boat on the way to the museum at the Yigal Allon Center

and round the boat, worrying, planning, fearing and, finally, speaking: "First we have to design the permanent stand, and then we have to place the boat on the new permanent stand and we must begin the work immediately, and…while it's still in the conservation pool…the base pipes have to be strung into the stand, then the stainless steel ribs have to be joined. Stainless steel legs have then to be manufactured to replace the metal legs and this will constitute the next step."

Every stage was emotion-filled and when it was completed, the joy was great and the confidence in their success rose in equal proportion.

The metal legs were dismantled, and the boat did not collapse, but stood proudly on all its 130 legs.

The entire "Order of the Boat" congregated, all dressed in their best white clothes and talking with each other in whispers. Orna, drafts of the boat in one hand, other papers in the other, all the time jotting down the results of calculations, was working out ways to prevent possible harm to the boat's frame.

Orna had made scrupulous plans for the day ahead. First, she had studied the operating mechanism of the crane. Then she had decided to build a protective frame around the boat to which the crane would connect, as she preferred for the crane to get a firm grip on the frame rather than on the boat itself. The entire team stood huddled around the boat, sending up a silent prayer for the crane to connect properly to the frame and transfer it safely to its permanent place.

The crane driver was nervous and tense, but, outwardly, he was calm and confident as he climbed up on the narrow metal strip until he reached its center, and did not become confused, did not lose his balance; he reached the center and joined the crane to the frame. Silence fell and all hearts prayed as one. No one uttered a breath and the crane, gripping the frame, very gradually lifted up the boat, which swung between the earth, the sea and the skies. The crane's arm made an almost complete circle, until it was above the opening into which it was meant to enter.

The crane driver surely did not breathe. The crane's arm stretched out and the boat began very slowly to enter the opening that had been prepared for it. Six agile people brought six large jacks. The crane driver lowered the boat carefully and accurately down onto them. Then the crane driver released his grip and the unbelievable happened. The boat stood, of its own accord, on all six jacks.

A bottle of champagne was cracked open. Here was a reason to celebrate.

But they still didn't know — only hoped — that the boat hadn't been damaged in the transfer.

People could hardly stand on their feet. Anxiety and tension gripped their souls and left everyone exhausted. Although they sighed in relief, they had reached a point of total physical and mental exhaustion.

Only Orna's words were audible: Tomorrow is a new day. Tomorrow at dawn, we shall see, at long last, if the transfer has been blessed with success.

With the first light on Sunday morning, the group gathered once again.

Feet walked in the direction of the Yigal Allon Center. Orna was already there. That night, she had not managed to fall asleep. Curiosity and anxiety led her to the Yigal Allon Center and even before the arrival of the members of the "Order of the Boat," she had started dismantling the packaging around the boat.

Very slowly, one more rib and another, one more part and then another part of the boat peeked out from inside the packaging and, what a wonder, the boat, undamaged, was revealed for all to see, standing there in its stainless steel cradle in all its glory. A joy for the eye to behold and the soul to enjoy.

They say that sometimes, when he wanted to get away from the adulation of the masses, he got into a boat and it was from there that he spoke to his followers — picture by Gustav Doche

The Miracle

With the spread of Christianity, there grew a love for the Holy Land and for the Sea of Galilee, particularly when it became widely known that Jesus' first field of activity was around this sea, for it was here that he encountered the first of his disciples, the fishermen, brothers Simon and Andrew, and Jacob and John, and asked them to lay down their nets. He believed that the fishermen had the talent to become fishers of hearts and souls. Even after his death, the Evangelists say that Jesus met with his disciples the fishermen on the fisherman's wharf at Tabha, where he gave Simon (called Peter) seniority over all his followers and said, "You shall guide my flock!" They say that sometimes, when he wanted to get away from the adulation of the masses, he would get into a boat and it was from there that he spoke to his followers.

For three years Jesus stayed in the region of the Sea of Galilee. He made his home in Caper-naum in the home of his disciple the fisherman Peter. From the port of Capernaum, he sailed in a fishing boat to visit the villages along the coast of the Sea of Galilee.

The herald of modern research into the Sea of Galilee region was a young Swede by the name of Fredric Hasselquist. In 1749, the daring young student set off on an adventure-filled journey of research. Unfortunately, the traveling proved to be too much for him, and he did not survive the return voyage. However, his notes were preserved and published posthumously as *Voyages and Travels in the Levant*. In fact the father of modern research was the Englishman Reverend Henry Baker Tristram, whose monumental book *The Flora and Fauna of the Holy Land* was published in 1884.

It was not only scientists, however, who took an interest in the Sea of Galilee. Religious leaders, too, like the Frankish Bishop Arculf, traveled here in 670 in search of the sources of the Jordan and explored the coast of the Sea of Galilee and its environs.

In the nineteenth century, the shores of the Kinneret were alive with activity. One of the more famous of the researchers in the region was John MacGregor, who conducted primary research in his boat, the *Rob Roy*, which has recently been transferred to Israel.

But from our point of view, it is the study conducted by the American oceanologist Edwin A. Link and his team that proves how great was the miracle that allowed a wooden boat to survive some two thousand years in sweet water. Link's 1960 archaeological expedition — the first to study the Sea of Galilee — focused mainly on the Hebrew Bible and the New Testament, and came to study those parts of the Sea of Galilee that are sacred to Christianity. They brought with them a small boat and the most sophisticated equipment (much of it designed by Link himself) in order to conduct an underwater study and excavation.

A team of the best divers in Israel joined them over a period of six weeks, and they dived and examined every inch of the depths near Capernaum and Magdala. They retrieved a large number of ceramic utensils, jugs and candles, and stone and copper tools from the Roman-Byzantine period, but, as is so often the case, the main discovery happened by chance.

The delegation's boat stopped due to a broken-down engine. They tried to repair the engine, jumped into the water to freshen up and, as usual, to search along the sea bed for interesting finds. And then they raised twenty-nine cooking pots which were subsequently dated to the first century BCE. Of the twenty-nine, seven were raised intact and it turned out that they had never been used. It appears that the wooden vessel that was transporting them had capsized and sunk in a storm, even before the merchant had managed to sell the pots.

Many long days were spent in the search for remains of the wooden boat, which had probably rotted away completely, for nothing was found. Only the boat's two anchors, which were made of stone, had survived. One of the anchors is on display in a museum in New York. The second anchor remains in Israel and is on display in the National Maritime Museum in Haifa. It weighs 21 kilograms (46.3 lbs.) and is made of flat, purplish basalt stone, 43 centimeters (17 in.) long; at its widest, it is 30 centimeters wide (11.8 in.) and is 13 centimeters (5 in.) thick at its thickest point. We have given this fact only to prove that *wooden boats do not survive for two thousand years in sweet water.*

A fortunate coincidence, fourteen years of strenuous and devoted labor, and a huge miracle had to take place in order for our boat to survive.

Epilogue

And Jacob loved Rachel, daughter of Laban, his mother's brother.

And Jacob served seven years for Rachel and they seemed but a few days.

And Laban gave to Jacob his daughter Leah, her older sister.

And Jacob served Laban a further seven years, those that followed, for Rachel.

Fourteen years Jacob served for Rachel and they seemed but a few days, because he loved Rachel.

And all the members of the "Order of the Boat" served for fourteen years, and they seemed but a few days, because of their love for the boat.

The ancient boat now at the Ygal Allon Center

From left to right: Kurt Raveh, Shelley Wachsmann, Moshe Lufan, Mendel Nun, Yuval Lufan

Part Two — The Region

The Cradle of Christianity

In the northern part of the Holy Land there lies a large inland sea that is special and wondrous: the Sea of Galilee. A number of locations around the sea make it unique. It is the main source of water for the State of Israel and has the most fascinating and exciting landscape, a focus of scientific interest. At its creation, fish — all kinds of fish — flowed into it from other continents, both far and near. And, besides this, the Sea of Galilee is the cradle of Christianity, the place in which Jesus preached from one fishing village to another, "told many things in parables," worked miracles, gathered his disciples and followers, helped the unfortunate and cured the sick. For almost two thousand years, the Sea of Galilee has been a lodestone for pilgrims and tourists. When you read Evangelist literature, you come closer to the Sea of Galilee, a two-thousand-year-old boat and Jesus.

"Now when Jesus saw great crowds around him, he gave orders to go over to the other side" (Matthew 8:18). Further on the apostle continues: "And when he got into the boat, his disciples followed him. A gale arose on the lake, so great that the boat was being swamped by the waves; but he was asleep. And they went and woke him up, saying, 'Lord, save us! We are perishing!' And he said to them, 'Why are you afraid, you of little faith?' Then he got up and rebuked the winds and the sea; and there was a dead calm. They were amazed, saying, 'What sort of man is this, that even the winds and the sea obey him?'" (Matthew 8:23–27).

These chapters inflamed the imagination of many people wherever they were read. And the most amazing expression of this is Rembrandt's famous 1633 painting, *Christ in the Storm on the*

Christ in the Storm on the Sea of Galilee, by Rembrandt

Sea of Galilee. Throughout the Gospels, there are descriptions of Jesus and his work around the Sea of Galilee. In the Gospel according to Matthew: "And after getting into a boat he crossed the water and came to his own town" (Mathew 9:1). Further on: "That same day Jesus went out of the house and sat beside the lake. Such great crowds gathered around him that he got into a boat and sat there, while the whole crowd stood on the beach" (Matthew: 13:1–2).

During the years 1983, 1984 and 1985 the Land of Israel knew a very heavy drought. The water level of the Sea of Galilee dropped drastically and virtually ran away from the shoreline. And two brothers, who were fishermen, sons of a fisherman father called Yanky (Jacob) Lufan, had gone around all their lives with a feeling that one day the Sea of Galilee would smile upon them and yield up to them a treasure. And here, during those drought years, Moshe and Yuval Lufan found a wooden boat, covered with mud and silt, as if a giant hand had taken it upon itself to save it from the sweet waters of the Sea of Galilee, so that the two brothers could restore and preserve it and show the whole world the greatest archaeological find of the twentieth century.

For years the two brothers worked, alongside large numbers of dedicated volunteers; it was hard work, full of love and determination and wisdom. And still, it is a huge kind of miracle that the boat survived for two thousand years, to be exhibited today in the Bet Allon Museum in Kibbutz Ginosar, pulling at the heartstrings and exciting the eyes of everyone who comes to see it.

And everyone who leaves Bet Allon after visiting the ancient boat can drive northward along the coast of the Sea of Galilee and arrive at the valley of Tabgha.

The valley of Tabgha was a valley teeming with people and activity. It was here that Jesus met the first of his disciples, a couple of fishermen brothers — Simon and Andrew, and another pair of fishermen brothers — Jacob and John. When Jesus met the two pairs of fishermen brothers, he called upon them to leave their fishing nets and, instead of seeking fish, to fish for the hearts of people. And they left their fathers and their fishing nets and followed Jesus.

When Jesus wanted to get away for a while from his many followers, he would climb up to the top of a mount overlooking Tabgha, where he found the solitude necessary to meditate and pray.

The church to commemorate the Sermon on the Mount was built next to the octagonal pool on the sharp rise on the way leading to Capernaum. This rise is known as the Mountain of the Beatitudes. It was here that Jesus taught his Sermon on the Mount, as related by Matthew: "When Jesus saw the crowds, he went up the mountain…. And he began to speak, and taught them, saying: 'Blessed are the poor

in spirit, for theirs is the kingdom of heaven….'" (Matthew 5:1–3). The third through eleventh verses of the sermon begin with the words "Blessed are…," hence the name Beatitude, which means "blessing" in Latin.

The Mountain of the Beatitudes is also said to be the place where Jesus chose his twelve disciples: "Now during those days he went out to the mountain to pray…. And when day came, he called his disciples and chose twelve of them, whom he also named apostles" (Luke 6:12–13).

A miraculous event believed to have occurred

at Tabgha is the third appearance of Jesus after his death, as related in John 21: "Just after daybreak, Jesus stood on the beach; but the disciples did not know that it was Jesus.… Simon Peter went aboard and hauled the net ashore, full of large fish.… Jesus said to them, 'Come and have breakfast.' …This was now the third time that Jesus appeared to the disciples after he was raised from the dead. When they had finished breakfast, Jesus said to Simon Peter, 'Simon son of John, do you love me more than these?' He said to him,

'Yes, Lord….' Jesus said to him, 'Feed my lambs'" (John 21:4, 11–12, 14–15).

After this event Peter's primacy was recognized. Later, according to Christian tradition, this spot is also the place at which Jesus practiced the miracle of the loaves and the fishes.

In the middle of the fourth century, the first churches were built in the Holy Land on the places where Jesus had been. In the Tabgha valley, churches were built to commemorate the important events. The first churches were simple,

Church of the Beatitudes

modest structures, and only in the fourth century were the modest buildings replaced by impressive basilicas. In late fourth century, when the simple building at Tabgha was replaced by a church, it included the traditional stone known as the Mensa Christi (Jesus' table), on which, according to tradition, Jesus and the disciples ate a meal of grilled fish around a fire.

During the Persian invasion of the region, the church was destroyed, and rebuilt, then destroyed again. Several times the pilgrims built a kind of wall, whose remains have been excavated and can be found near the new church that now stands in the middle of the traditional site. In 1935, the Franciscans built the new church, which includes within it the remains of the original Church of the Primacy of St. Peter.

The Church of the Multiplication of the Loaves and Fishes was built to commemorate the miracle in which Jesus fed five thousand people with five loaves of bread and two fish (Matthew 14:13–21; Mark 6:30–44; John 6: 1–14). It, too, was built near the octagonal pool. The first church was built in the sixth century as a typical basilica with a central nave and two aisles. The rock under the altar in the main hall of the church is said to be the rock on which Jesus laid the loaves and the fish. The church is especially famous for its multicolored mosaic floors, with illustrations of the basket, containing the loaves and the two fish. Other tiles depict peacocks (symbol of eternity),

lotus flowers and other plants. The mosaics have been very well preserved and are among the loveliest in the Holy Land. When the ancient church was discovered during excavations, the owners of the area — the order of the Benedictine monks — built a new church over it in 1935.

Settlement of the Galilee Region

The Sea of Galilee is situated deep in the Jordan Great Rift Valley, which is part of the Afro-Syrian Rift Valley that crosses the Land of Israel from north to south. The Afro-Syrian Rift Valley begins in northern Syria and ends in Africa and is the deepest of all the world's rift valleys. The Jordan Great Rift Valley is a weak point in the earth's crust and its cracks have not yet completely healed. Proof of this are the many hot mineral springs that burst out of the earth along the length of the valley, especially around the Sea of Galilee.

Remains of the oldest settlement in the land and, indeed, in the entire world (outside of Africa) were discovered in Ubeidiya, three kilometers south of the Sea of Galilee, near Kibbutz Bet-Zera. The inhabitants of this ancient settlement survived by hunting wild carnivorous animals

The mosaic of the loaves and fishes

(especially hippopotamus) and gathering berries and other forms of vegetation.

The first inhabitants of the Sea of Galilee region consisted of small groups of fishermen and gatherers of food. Their way of life is revealed by their kitchen waste, which contained mainly the bones of venison and fish. Further proof of the ties forged by man and his place of residence is

the fact that these people made a habit of burying their dead close to where they lived. At an excavation in Ein Gev on the Sea of Galilee, the archaeologists, Dudik Ben-Ami and Uri Fuchter, found the folded skeleton of a thirty-year-old woman, along with a basalt mortar and pestle, discovered in the vicinity of the female skeleton.

This mortar and pestle was obviously used

in grinding seeds, testimony to man's changing eating habits and, in fact, to the beginning of organized agriculture; man developed ties to the land and virtually stopped his nomadic way of life. The newly agricultural dwellers reaped the wild wheat with the help of a sickle carved out of flint and used the ground grains to make themselves a kind of porridge, which preceded the bread we know today. This mortar and pestle and the female skeleton are on permanent exhibition in the Israel Museum in Jerusalem.

An important change took place in man's lifestyle during the fourth millenium BCE. Man invented the boat and began sailing the seas. And it was during this period that the first permanent

The mosaic of the peacocks and lotus flowers

settlements were established along the coast of the Sea of Galilee.

All Around the Sea of Galilee Coast

The stretch of coastland that surrounds much of the Sea of Galilee is narrow; only at the estuaries of the rivers flowing into the lake does the water body push itself inwards to make room for the valleys that provide a door to the rivers. The largest valleys are those of the Batiha and the Ginosar. The importance of the Sea of Galilee springs from its potential for agricultural development and from the fact that even in earliest times, it provided a crossroads between continents — internationally, too, and not merely a land-bound intersection, but also a meeting of paths that connected the north with the south and the west with the east.

The Sea of Galilee and the sea traffic that traveled on it provided a convenient shortcut and much use was made of it.

The Batiha valley, the largest of the Galilee's valleys, consists of many rivulets converging into four main rivers. The rivulets of the Batiha valley descend from the center of the Golan Heights, at a height of 800–1000 meters (2600–3300 ft.),

down to the Sea of Galilee, which lies 210 meters (690 ft.) below sea level. The rivulets provide a powerful stream of water, so that, even two thousand years ago, the whole region was a bustling hubbub of life. Advanced agricultural methods were developed; raised pools were built, into which waters from the melting snows flowed fiercely and produced power that created energy. The waters fell on flour mills, turned wheels and ground wheat.

Bethsaida

The first town to be built in the Batiha valley was Bethsaida, which was originally a fishing village. King Herod's son, Philip, raised Bethsaida to municipal status in the year 4 CE. He began by extending the site of the town, after which a large number of new inhabitants flowed in. Philip then renamed the town "Julias," after the daughter of the Roman Augustus Caesar, his close friend and confidant.

Jesus chose to spend time in Bethsaida because it came under the auspices of Philip, whose regime was more tolerant than that of his tyrannical, suspicious brother Herod Antipas. Here Jesus preached, healed the sick and worked his miracles, and because of this Bethsaida grew in fame. Three of Jesus' disciples, Simon Peter, Andrew and Philip were born and raised in Bethsaida and it was somewhere near Bethsaida that Jesus worked his miracle of the loaves and fishes, whereby he fed five thousand people who had gathered to listen to him, with five loaves of bread and two fishes. Since the actual location of this site is not certain, Christian tradition has removed the miracle to Tabgha, west of the Sea of Galilee.

There are various assumptions regarding the location of Bethsaida, the most feasible of which is that Julias was built on a mount known as et-Tell, some three kilometers (a little under two miles) distant from the fishing village on the estuary of the Zaki. Further details to authenticate this assumption can be found in *The Jewish War* by the Jewish historian Josephus, according to whom the mount of et-Tell is closer to the Jordan River than to the Sea of Galilee.

The Roman historian Pliny completes this by saying that the Jordan empties into a lake surrounded by beautiful towns, such as Tiberias on the western side and Julias and Hippos to the east. The main finds on the mount of et-Tell are the foundations of houses, although impressive remains are yet to be discovered. Recently, it has been found that Bet-Habek stands at the center of a broad tel, one of whose sides was destroyed and covered by water and the other sunk in a swamp. The most obvious remaining architectural feature

is a staircase leading to a large building consisting of several stories. Its bricks were stolen and only a large pit remains under the staircase. The waves of the Sea of Galilee revealed the foundations of a seven-meter-wide round tower.

Kursi — Country of the Gadarenes

Of all the locations along the coast of the Sea of Galilee, the best place on which to establish a fishing village was at the estuary of the River Semech. The large stone bank that surrounds the estuary provides the best fishing grounds for the famous Sea of Galilee sardines. The little sardines attract the larger fish, which come to feed on them, and, thus, the best fishing grounds are created. It is no coincidence that this river is called Semech; in the ancient alphabet of Aramaic and Hebrew, languages that dominated the region in ancient times, the letter *samech* is thought to have derived from "fish." In the twenty-first century, most of the people inhabiting the region of the Sea of Galilee are unaware that two thousand years ago their predecessors enjoyed a safe harbor right next to this rich fishing ground. Today, the remains of this harbor can be seen north of Tel Kursi.

Kursi, like its close neighbors Bethsaida and

Capernaum, is known as the place in which, according to early Christian tradition, Jesus miraculously caused the demons that had taken hold of a man to enter the bodies of pigs grazing on the nearby hill. The pigs ran wildly into the Sea of Galilee and were drowned (Matthew 8:28–32; Luke 8:26–33).

The identification of the place of the miracle with the village of Kursi, which is also known as Gadarenes (Matthew 8:28) or Gerasenes (Luke 8:26), was established by early Christian writers and pilgrims, among them Mar Saba and his pupils, who prayed at the site in the year 491 CE.

According to Cyril of Seythopolis, the Roman name for Beth Shean, Saba and his pupils first came to the eastern coast of the Sea of Galilee, to Kursi, where they prayed, and only later did they cross the sea to the place of the seven springs, which is known today as Tabgha. These prayers are the first sign of the existence of a church in Kursi. In 723 a pilgrim visited the spot on which Jesus cured the man who had been suffering from demons, and he recorded that the Christians had a church on the spot.

The most interesting testimony is that of Mendel Nun, who described how, in 1970, when work began on a new road to the Golan Heights, workers noticed remains from the Byzantine period lying on the side of the road at the entrance to the river estuary. All road work stopped immediately and was replaced by an archeological dig

to rescue the remains. The dig uncovered a fifth-century church and monastery.

The compound was surrounded by a wall and entered from the west, the direction of the Sea of Galilee, through the main gate which was flanked by a tower. In front of the church was an atrium (over which the new road was to have run) paved with flagstones and surrounded by columns. The church was built as a basilica with a nave on either side of the central hall. Around the apse in the eastern wall were stone benches for the clergy. On both sides of the apse were rooms, the one on the south being a baptistery. The floor of the church was covered with beautifully colorful mosaics, some of which are well preserved. Under the chapel, on the southern side of the main hall, was a crypt in which thirty skeletons, presumably of Byzantine monks, were buried. The site was carefully excavated and restored in the 1970s and is now an important tourist attraction.

Mendel Nun, who was involved in the excavation, was thus responsible for saving an important historical site. The new road was redirected to a point away from the site. Over three seasons of archeological excavation, the first two under the directorship of Danny Orman and the third under Vasilius Tsafiris, all that remains of the ancient church was revealed, including the monastery's walls and gate, and several of the monks' residential quarters on the northern side of the courtyard. The fifth-century monastery in

Kursi was built half a kilometer from the fishing village on the coast and is the largest one found in the Land of Israel. It suffered severe damage at the beginning of the seventh century, apparently during the Persian invasion.

The quayside at Kursi is located at the center of installations typical of a fishing village. For example, to the north of the quay, you can see the remains of a square pool, 1.25 meters (4 ft.) above ground level, with inside measurements of 3 meters by 3.5 meters (9.8×11.5 ft.). The pool had been plastered on the inside and was used for storing the larger fish caught by the local fishermen. The pool received a constant flow of water, which allowed it to keep the fish alive until the wholesalers arrived to buy them. The surprising thing is that the water that flowed into the pool was not seawater, but water that came down via a ceramic pipeline from a small aqueduct created by the Semech River.

A platform was built near the pool, to which the wholesalers arrived to buy their fish.

In order to keep the fish fresh, the fishermen tied to their boats a crate in which holes had been made. This was sunk in the

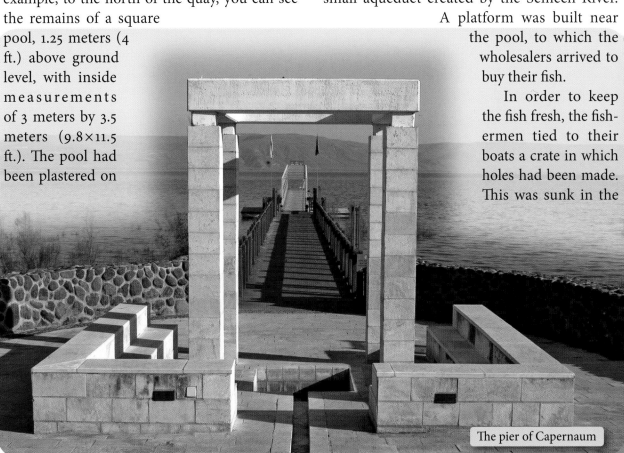

The pier of Capernaum

water and dragged behind the boat; the fishermen placed their freshly caught fish in it and brought their catch in to port, still alive.

Capernaum

Capernaum was an ancient fishing town on the northwestern shore of the Sea of Galilee, uninhabited since the eighth century. Jesus settled here after he left Nazareth, and it was the place where he made his first disciples from among the humble local fishermen — Simon (who was called Peter) and his brother, Andrew, as well as James and his brother John. Exactly at the same time as Jesus began traveling through the Galilee, from one fishing village to another, Capernaum was a medium-sized settlement on the Sea of Galilee, famous for the quality of the wheat that grew in the fields nearby. In that region, the Sea of Galilee was rich in various species of fish and, of course, most of the inhabitants of Capernaum made their living from fishing and agriculture.

In fact, before the town of Tiberias became well known, Capernaum was an important location for commerce, fishing and agriculture and it even boasted a customs house. Bethsaida and Capernaum shared agricultural and family ties. When Simon met a relative of his in Capernaum,

he married her and went to live with his parents-in-law. Jesus, on his travels between the various fishing villages, met Simon's mother-in-law and healed her of her illness. He then went to live in Simon's mother-in-law's home.

Jesus traveled around the fishing villages and, when he had completed his journeys, he returned to Capernaum, which became his home base and the place from which he set off on his journeys around the villages surrounding the Sea of Galilee. "Again he began to teach beside the sea. Such a very large crowd gathered around him that he got into a boat on the sea and sat there, while the whole crowd was beside the sea on the land. He began to teach them many things in parables…" (Mark 4:1–2). We learn from this that when he taught the people on dry land and the people gathered and crowded around him, Jesus preferred to get into a boat on the Sea of Galilee, and, by doing so, release some of the pressure on him.

"Jesus departed with his disciples to the sea, and a great multitude from Galilee followed him; hearing all that he was doing, they came to him in great numbers from Judea, Jerusalem, Idumea, beyond the Jordan, and the region around Tyre and Sidon. He told his disciples to have a boat ready for him because of the crowd, so that they would not crush him" (Mark 3:7–9). The boat served Jesus as a shield against the masses and provided him with a comfortable vehicle with which to travel from village to village.

Capernaum was located close to the international sea road. The road led to Capernaum from the vale of Ginosar and then the "sea road" distanced itself from the Sea of Galilee and, from Korazim River, it led up, northward. It was an international road which joined north to south and west to east and was an important factor in the town's economic development during the middle of the first century CE.

Among the recorded teachings of Jesus at Capernaum were many parables, such as that of the sower, of tares among the wheat, of a grain of mustard seed, of leaven, of the treasure hidden in the field and of the fishing net (Matthew 13). Because of his preaching and the many miracles he performed, large crowds of people from Capernaum and the vicinity flocked around Jesus and formed the nucleus of one of the earliest congregations of converts to the new religion. The town of Capernaum thus played a major role at the very beginning of Christianity.

Several dwellings from the first century BCE have been excavated; of special significance is the House of Peter. Between the first century BCE and the fourth century CE, this was a common, poor residence, with several rooms grouped around an irregular courtyard. One of the rooms was distinguished by a better floor, or rather a succession of floors of crushed limestone and painted plaster coat-

ing on the walls. In the second stage, in the first half of the fourth century, this room became the center of a building surrounded by a wall and thus secluded from the town. The room now had a roof supported by an arch. This may have been the church seen by the nun Egeria. In the middle of the fifth century this building was leveled and an octagonal church built on the site. It had a mosaic floor, part of which — including a peacock centerpiece — can still be seen. Although there is nothing in the early house to identify its owner, its development into a fully recognized church indicates a strong tradition connecting it

Capernaum — the new church on the ruins of the home of St. Peter

with Peter and with the activities of Jesus in Capernaum.

Franciscan monks, who excavated the site recently, found the remains of fishing lines on the floor of the house and writing on the wall in Aramaic and Greek, probably written by second- and third-century Christian pilgrims. The Franciscan monks, who own the site, also uncovered the living quarters in the area between the ancient synagogue and the church. They discovered interesting facts about the day-to-day lives of the inhabitants.

Each building housed one extended family. The house was built around a large inner courtyard, where the family carried out its daily life. A stove stood in the courtyard, together with grinding stones and a mortar and pestle. In the courtyard, the people ground their wheat and baked their bread, cooked their food and carried out all their other activities. The rooms were located all around the courtyard — narrow and dark and doorless. In the winter the inhabitants slept in the rooms, but in the unbearable heat of summer, the family would climb the stairs and sleep on the roof, which was certainly cooler and better aired.

There was only one door, which led from the courtyard to the street and was locked each evening. Capernaum was a town that was not surrounded by a wall. The Romans used it as a garrison town and kept it under siege, but did not wage war against it. Thus, although it was unharmed by wars or rebellions, there was no real feeling of security in Capernaum, and its inhabitants gradually abandoned it during the first century CE.

Roman Building Techniques

The Romans were wonderful builders who incorporated amazing new innovations in their building methods. They were the first people in history to create concrete. The secret of Roman concrete was its cement, which contained volcanic dust, readily available in Italy because of the many active volcanoes, such as Mount Vesuvius. Roman concrete was made by mixing secret quantities of cement and limestone with volcanic dust and ground organic material, to which were added small stones to form a strong material that hardened quickly, even under water. Ordinary cement, on the other hand, is made of burnt limestone, sand and water, and is only able to harden once the water has evaporated.

To this day, engineers stand in awe at the site of Roman buildings; they were the first to build arches and the first to include long archways in their buildings.

The ancient Romans were also the first to build aqueducts for delivering fresh spring water directly to their homes. They built an aqueduct, called Aqua-Claudia, 70 kilometers (43 mi.) long with 30-meter-high arches. They built an aqueduct that was among the longest on earth, the winding aqueduct of Augustus, which was known as the Matrix and which provided water to nine towns around the bay of Naples. According to A. Trevor Hodge, who wrote *Roman Aqueducts and Water Supply*, the Roman-built water supply system in the first century CE supplied much more water to the city of Rome than did the water system supplying water to the city of New York in 1985.

They built the Pantheon, which in Latin means "temple of all the Gods," but which has been a Christian church since the seventh century. This best-preserved of all Roman buildings and the oldest important building in the world still has its original roof intact. It was built in honor of the Emperor

The Greek Orthodox church at Capernaum

Hadrian. The height to the oculus is 43.58 meters (143 ft.), and the diameter of the interior circle is 43.28 meters (142 ft.). All the visitors and pilgrims who make their way to the Pantheon stand before it speechless, unable to understand what it is that supports the dome in such a way as to protect it from collapsing — completely mocking all the laws of nature.

Thus were the ancient Roman building techniques; and all the ancient ports that were used two thousand years ago around the coast of the Sea of Galilee were built by the Romans. The early Christian explorers who came to seek the remains of the ancient ports from the days of Jesus were unable to find them simply because they lacked sufficient archeological and underwater knowledge and they were not familiar with the character of the Sea of Galilee.

The first people to find the remains of the ancient ports were members of the Society for Marine Archeological Research, Avner Raban and Yehoshua Shapira.

A general overview of the shore of the Sea of Galilee shows us that the people who lived in the region about two thousand years ago knew how to design and build sophisticated harbors and quays. Each harbor was designed to accommodate the wind cycles at each particular part of the coast as well as the shape of the coast at each particular location. They knew how to economize on construction costs, and to build stone breakwaters parallel to the Sea of Galilee shore to protect it from erosion by waves (walls constructed underwater and extending above the highest level of the tide by two feet), and to complete the necessary depth by deepening the harbor.

The base of the breakwater is usually sunk to a depth of between -212 and -211 meters (-695.5 to -692.3 ft.), and only the edges reached a depth of -213 meters (-698.8 ft.) in order for the breakwater to withstand the pressure of the waves that beat on it. The breakwater, at its base, was 4–6 meters (13.1–19.7 ft.), as compared to the upper part which was only 2–3 meters (6.6–9.8 ft.). The height of the breakwater (it must be assumed) reached a height of 3–3.5 meters (9.8–11.5 ft.) and was built of large basalt and chalk stones, and its building was very accurate. The builders of the breakwater knew how to build areas that were comfortable for anchoring boats and to determine the best locations for an easy entry for the boats.

A surprising detail was discovered, for example, at the harbor at Susita, in the form of a small protrusion emerging from the edge of the breakwater into the Sea of Galilee. This protrusion was meant to serve as a deep water quay, on which travelers could embark and disembark the boats, and thus save the boat master the trouble of having to enter the harbor through a narrow opening.

Magdala — Migdal

One example of a sophisticated port city is Magdala, which was an important agricultural, fishing and trade center at the junction of the road coming north from Tiberias and the Via Maris coming from the Lower Galilee into the fertile plain of Gennesaret, the town of "Mary, called Magdalene" (Luke 8:2). Magdala was also renowned as a center for flax weaving and dyeing, and the robes worn by Jesus at the time of his crucifixion are said to have been made there.

All the historical sources agree that there was a large port at Magdala. Today, when the water level of the Sea of Galilee has dropped, its remains are revealed. Anyone familiar with the wind cycles over the Sea of Galilee knows that the westerly wind, the one that causes the waves to rise and froth, bursts into the region from the estuary of the Arbel River west of Magdala. But because of the simple fact that Magdala is very close to the shore and the wind is still at the beginning of its journey into the middle of the Sea of Galilee, it is still not powerful enough at that stage to whip up the waves, so that the waters near the port of Magdala are calm and pleasant for anchoring.

In 1960, the American oceanologist Edwin A. Link discovered a section of a concrete floor in Migdal. It was cast in a way that made it very strong and managed to survive the beating of two thousand years' worth of waves. The concrete floor was discovered at a depth of several meters below the level of the Sea of Galilee. Link believed that the floor is what remains of a quay belonging to the ancient port of Magdala. The main structure of the port has not yet been discovered.

In fact, the port of Magdala is built in two sections: the first consists of the quayside and the second of a protected pool. At first, the archeologists believed that these were the remains of a Roman road. But further examination revealed another section, and then it became clear that the two parts differ from each other and are not at the same height. One was 211 meters (692.3 ft.) below sea level, while the other was -211.2 (692.9 ft.) and it is clear that this was not a Roman road. Moreover, remains of a wall that supported the surfaces of the various heights of quays are clearly visible.

North of the quays, the shoreline of the Sea of Galilee withdrew inward and created a small bay, in which the port's protected area was constructed, sheltered by a tall breakwater that can withstand the waves that flow in from the east. The two parts of the port of Magdala constitute the largest port excavated to date, and confirm the sources, according to which large numbers of boats came there to anchor.

Magdala experienced its most prosperous times during the Roman period in the Land of Israel, exactly at the time that Jesus traveled among the fishing villages surrounding the Sea of Galilee.

The town of Magdala was established during the Hellenistic period (after 300 BCE) and was known as Migdal Nunya, or Migdal of the fishes. Josephus refers to Migdal by its Greek name, Tarichaeae, which literally means "salting fish." These names are evidence that Magdala was a center for preserving fish.

Preserved fish were among the better known exports of the Holy Land. According to the Roman historian Strabo, Rome of the first century CE was a highly populated city, and many Romans waited with baited anticipation for a ship to arrive from Migdala bearing a cargo of fish from the Sea of Galilee, which were considered even then to be the best to be had. And today, too, at the beginning of the twenty-first century, in the modern city of Tel Aviv in the State of Israel, one feels very much like the ancient Romans with their love of fish from the Sea of Galilee.